The ICSA **Remuneration Committee Guide**

The ICSA

Remuneration Committee Guide

Sean O'Hare
Remuneration Committee Institute

SPONSORED BY KPMG LLP (UK)

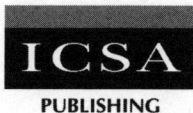

ICSA
PUBLISHING

Published by ICSA Publishing Ltd
16 Park Crescent
London W1B 1AH

Typeset by Paul Barrett Book Production, Cambridge
Printed in Great Britain by TJ International Ltd, Padstow, Cornwall

British Library Cataloguing in Publication Data
A catalogue record for this book is available from the British Library

ISBN   1-86072-333-0
ISBN 13   978-1-86072-333-9

Contents

Preface

Corporate governance excellence continues to be an important element of UK business. The expectations of stakeholders in the corporate governance process, including the process of setting executive remuneration, have never been higher, and scrutiny by investors never more stringent. As a consequence, remuneration issues continue to dominate the corporate governance landscape in the UK, as indeed they have for the past decade. Whereas public shareholder anger was once a rarity, nowadays significant votes against the Director's Remuneration Report are increasingly common. As a result, the role of the Remuneration Committee has increased in terms of its responsibility to its stakeholders, and its processes have become somewhat more onerous as a result.

Recognising that effective corporate governance is a cornerstone of shareholder protection, initiatives by regulators and stakeholders to help shape and guide corporate governance practices have confirmed the Remuneration Committee's key role in corporate governance and oversight. The Financial Reporting Council's revised Combined Code and the related guidance for Remuneration Committees (Higgs guidance and Greenbury) contain recommendations designed to strengthen the effectiveness of Remuneration Committees, clarify and enhance their oversight roles, and enhance their accountability for the setting of an executive remuneration process.

Charged with setting executive remuneration, Remuneration Committees find themselves trying to balance the expectations of executives with the needs of the company and its shareholders. Unfortunately this challenge is not always met with success. If you are seen to pay too much, then you will have failed the 'appropriateness' test laid down by shareholders and can expect them to protest through the use of their votes at the next general meeting. Alternatively, if you fail to offer enough incentive, you run the risk of losing the most critical employees upon whom the success of the company is based.

As with most things in life, there is no right answer as such, but the Remuneration Committee Institute (RCI) believes that a properly constituted Remuneration Committee with sufficient authority and independence of mind will be well placed to meet the challenge of attracting and retaining the right talent and, ultimately, of motivating them to deliver real shareholder value.

This book identifies current and emerging issues that Remuneration Committees should be aware of, and react to, and describes Remuneration Committee practices that can provide the support and structure necessary in fulfilling their terms of reference. We at the RCI believe all Remuneration Committees can benefit from comparing their practices against those described in this publication in their effort to critique, tailor and improve the ways in which they operate.

In today's complex and evolving business environment a Remuneration Committee that operates effectively is a key feature in a strong corporate governance culture and can bring significant benefits to a company. We hope this publication will help ensure that Remuneration Committees achieve their objectives and thereby add value to the board of directors, their organisation and its stakeholders.

We owe our thanks to those who have supported the Remuneration Committee Institute since its formation in 2004. We believe this book will help Remuneration Committee members meet the challenges demanded of them by providing genuinely practical guidance. Our thanks in particular to David Snell and Nicola Collins, without whose efforts this book could not have been produced.

Sean O'Hare
Chairman, Remuneration Committee Institute,
sponsored by KPMG LLP (UK)

About the Remuneration Committee Institute

While the work of the Remuneration Committee is scrutinised ever more closely by investors and the media, developments in corporate governance, accounting, tax and disclosure regulations over recent years have made its work increasingly complicated. Recognising these developments, the Remuneration Committee Institute (RCI) has been created to assist Remuneration Committee members in keeping pace with their changing role. Sponsored by KPMG LLP (UK), the Remuneration Committee Institute is a sister organisation of the Audit Committee Institute and provides a forum to foster the exchange of ideas and experience, as well as a resource to which members can turn for information or to share knowledge, experience and ideas. The RCI can be reached via email at remunerationcommittee@kpmg.co.uk.

For more information, please contact:

Nicola Collins
Remuneration Committee Institute
KPMG LLP (UK)
1–2 Dorset Rise
London
EC4Y 8EN

Introduction

Shaping the remuneration committee agenda

The role of those responsible for corporate governance, and the setting of executive remuneration, continue to face intense scrutiny by regulators, legislators, institutional investors and the general public. Attention is focused not only on the board of directors but also on those committees that have been delegated responsibility and accountability by the board. Remuneration Committees are clearly viewed as a critical component of the overall corporate governance process. Accordingly, many Remuneration Committees are examining the nature and extent of their roles, members' qualifications and independence, and their interaction and involvement with the performance evaluation process.

Effective Remuneration Committees are supported by fundamental 'building blocks' – an appropriate structure and foundation, reasonable and well-defined responsibilities, and an understanding of current and emerging issues. Only through carefully designed practices can a Remuneration Committee maximise its contribution to an organisation. Remuneration Committees need to understand these building blocks and the specific practices that can be used in implementing governance activities. By comparing practices currently being performed to leading practices, Remuneration Committees can identify and select a set of practices as the most effective and efficient in its particular circumstances. This book describes such practices.

Remuneration Committees have evolved from ad hoc committees with few defined responsibilities to what they are today: critical committees with growing responsibilities that are accountable to the board of directors, and ultimately to shareholders.

Brought to prominence in 1995 through Sir Richard Greenbury's report on *Directors' Remuneration*, the duties of Remuneration Committees have grown with successive corporate governance reports. These culminated in the Financial Reporting Council's revised *Combined Code on Corporate Governance* (see Appendix 1) and the related guidance for non-executive directors by Sir Derek Higgs, issued in 2003.

Greenbury, Higgs and the Combined Code are all designed to assist boards in making suitable corporate governance arrangements. Although specific practices are not mandated, the Financial Services Authority's Listing Rules require companies incorporated within the UK to report on how they apply the 14 corporate governance principles and 21 supporting principles included in the Combined Code, and to confirm the extent of their compliance with the 48 detailed Combined Code provisions, explaining the rationale behind any non-compliance.

Using this book

This book starts by looking at the role of the Remuneration Committee as set out by the revised Combined Code. The chapters that follow look at how to create an effective Remuneration Committee, and then how to run that committee. The last chapter discusses the responsibilities of the Remuneration Committee.

For the convenience of readers, many of the documents contained in the appendices are reproduced on the accompanying CD so that they may easily be adapted to suit individual requirements.

1 The role of the Remuneration Committee

Public and shareholder concerns over the excesses of directors' remuneration in the 1990s, particularly in privatised utility industries, led to Sir Richard Greenbury being charged with leading a study group to identify good practice in determining directors' remuneration and prepare a Code of such practice for use by UK PLCs. Many of Greenbury's recommendations have filtered through into the Directors' Remuneration Report Regulations 2002 (DRR Regs – see Appendix 2) and the FRC's Combined Code.

Ten years later and directors' pay was once again in the spotlight. Excessive executive compensation was cited as a cause of the corporate scandals at Enron and WorldCom. The role of the non-executive director, once again, had been catapulted into the spotlight. In the US the response was to form the Commission on Public Trust and Private Enterprise. The Commission made recommendations to combat out-of-control CEO remuneration and the use of stock options. Here in the UK, the Government undertook a consultation on directors' remuneration, resulting in the DRR Regulations. A few years later Sir Derek Higgs concluded his work on the role of the non-executive director, and the revised Combined Code was issued.

The following sets out the principles and provisions relating to the Remuneration Committee contained in the revised Combined Code.

Code Principles

No one other than the committee chairman and members is entitled to be present at a meeting of the nomination, audit or remuneration committee, but others may attend at the invitation of the committee (Principle A.3).

The chairman should ensure that the directors continually update their skills and the knowledge and familiarity with the company as required to fulfil their role on both the board and board committees. The company should provide the necessary resources for developing and updating its directors' knowledge and capabilities (Principle A.5).

All directors should be submitted for re-election at regular intervals, subject to continued satisfactory performance. The board should ensure planned and progressive refreshing of the Board (Principle A.7).

Levels of remuneration should be sufficient to attract, retain and motivate directors of the quality required to run the company successfully, but a company should avoid paying more than is necessary for this purpose. A significant proportion of executive directors' remuneration should be structured so as to link rewards to corporate and individual performance (Principle B.1).

The Remuneration Committee should judge where to position their company relative to other companies. However, they should use such comparisons with caution, in view of the risk of an upward ratchet of remuneration levels with no corresponding improvement in performance. They should also be sensitive to pay and employment conditions elsewhere in the group, especially when determining annual salary increases (Supporting Principle B.1).

There should be a formal and transparent procedure for developing policy on executive remuneration and for fixing the remuneration packages of individual directors. No director should be involved in deciding his or her own remuneration (Principle B.2).

The remuneration committee should consult the chairman and/or chief executive about their proposals relating to the remuneration of other executive directors. The Remuneration Committee should also be responsible for appointing any consultants in respect of executive director remuneration. Where executive directors or senior management are involved in advising or supporting the Remuneration Committee, care should be taken to recognise and avoid conflicts of interest (Supporting Principle B.2).

Code Provisions

The board should ensure that directors, especially non-executive directors, have access to independent professional advice at the company's expense where they judge it necessary to discharge their responsibilities as directors. Committees should be provided with sufficient resources to undertake their duties (Provision A.5.2).

All directors should have access to the advice and services of the company secretary, who is responsible to the board for ensuring that board procedures are complied with. Both the appointment and removal of the company secretary should be a matter for the board as a whole (Provision A.5.3).

The board should state in the annual report how performance evaluation of the board, its committees and its individual directors has been conducted. The non-executive directors, led by the senior independent director, should be responsible for performance evaluation of the chairman, taking into account the views of executive directors (Provision A.6.1).

The performance-related elements of remuneration should form a significant proportion of the total remuneration package of executive directors and should be designed to align their interests with those of shareholders and to give these directors keen incentives to perform at the highest levels. In designing schemes of performance-related remuneration, the Remuneration Committee should follow the provisions in Schedule A to this code (Provision B.1.1).

The Remuneration Committee should consider carefully what compensation commitments (including pension contributions and all other elements) their directors' terms of appointment would entail in the event of early termination of office. The aim should be to avoid rewarding poor performance. They should take a robust line on reducing compensation to reflect departing directors' obligations to mitigate loss (Provision B.1.5).

The board should establish a Remuneration Committee of at least three, or in the case of smaller companies two, members, who should all be independent non-executive directors. The Remuneration Committee should make available its terms of reference, explaining its role and the authority delegated to it by the board. Where remuneration consultants are appointed, a statement should be made as to whether they have any other connection with the company (Provision B.2.1).

The Remuneration Committee should have delegated to it responsibility for setting remuneration for all executive directors and the chairman, including pension rights and any compensation payments. The committee should also recommend and monitor the level and structure of remuneration for senior management. The definition of 'senior management' for this purpose should be determined by the board, but should normally include the first layer of management below board level (Provision B.2.2).

The board itself, or, where required by the Articles of Association, the shareholders, should determine the remuneration of the non-executive directors within the limits set in the Articles of Association. Where permitted by the Articles, the board may however delegate this responsibility to a committee, which might include the chief executive (Provision B.2.3).

Schedule A – Combined Code

1 The Remuneration Committee should consider whether the directors should be eligible for annual bonuses. If so, performance conditions should be relevant, stretching and designed to enhance shareholder value. Upper limits should be set and disclosed. There may be a case for part payment in shares to be held for a significant period.

2 The Remuneration Committee should consider whether the directors should be eligible for benefits under long-term incentive schemes. Traditional share option schemes should be weighed against other kinds of long-term incentive scheme. In normal circumstances, shares granted or other forms of deferred remuneration should not vest, and options should not be exercisable, in less than three years. Directors should be encouraged to hold their shares for a further period after vesting or exercise, subject to the need to finance any costs of acquisition and associated tax liabilities.

3 Any new long-term incentive schemes which are proposed should be approved by shareholders and should preferably replace any existing schemes or at least form part of a well-considered overall plan, incorporating existing schemes. The total rewards potentially available should not be excessive.

4 Payouts or grants under all incentive schemes, including new grants under existing share option schemes, should be subject to challenging performance criteria reflecting the company's objectives. Consideration should be given to criteria which reflect the company's performance relative to a group of comparator companies in some key variables, such as total shareholder return.

5 Grants under executive share option and other long-term incentive schemes should normally be phased rather than awarded in one large block.

6 In general, only basic salary should be pensionable.

7 The remuneration committee should consider the pension consequences and associated costs to the company of basic salary increases and any other changes in pensionable remuneration, especially for directors close to retirement.

Listing Rules

It should be noted that the Listing Rules of the UK Listing Authority require UK-incorporated listed companies to include within their annual reports:

- a statement of how it has applied the Combined Code principles, providing sufficient explanation to enable its shareholders to evaluate properly how the principles have been applied; and
- a statement as to whether or not it has complied throughout the accounting period with the Combined Code provisions.

A company that has not complied with the Code provisions, or complied with only some of the Code provisions or (in the case of provisions whose requirements are of a continuing nature) has complied for only part of an accounting period, must specify the Code provisions with which it has not complied, and (where relevant) for what part of the period such non-compliance continued, and give reasons for any non-compliance.

2 Creating an effective Remuneration Committee

Remuneration Committees are established by boards of directors to help discharge their fiduciary responsibility. How the committee fulfils that mandate varies according to the clarity of the committee's mission, the abilities of the committee's members, and the tone set at the top of the governance structure. A Remuneration Committee that operates effectively is a key feature in a strong corporate governance culture and can bring significant benefits to the company.

In this chapter we present some of the characteristics that, based on our experience at the RCI, mark a strong and effective Remuneration Committee. These characteristics should be viewed not as elements carved in stone, but as components in a process that can – and should – be continually improved to enhance the committee's effectiveness.

Remuneration Committee composition

The Combined Code recommends that Remuneration Committees should comprise at least three independent non-executive directors (two, for companies outside the FTSE 350); however, the size of the Remuneration Committee will vary, depending upon the needs and culture of the company and the extent of delegated responsibilities to the committee. The objective is to allow the committee to function efficiently, all members to participate, and an appropriate level of diversity of experience and knowledge. Committees of three to six individuals are generally appropriate to achieve those objectives.

> The board should establish a remuneration committee of at least three, or in the case of smaller companies two members, who should all be independent non-executive directors.

Combined Code Provision B.2.1

Appointments to the Remuneration Committee should be made by the board on the recommendation of the Nomination Committee, in consultation with the Remuneration Committee chairman. The appointment of non-executive directors on three-year terms, with staggered expiration dates to ensure continuity, is common in business today. Many companies have no set policies for rotating committee members but depend on weighing a member's experience against the risks of complacency. Without a rotation policy, it is important for the board of directors to evaluate a Remuneration Committee member's performance to see that it meets both the board's and the committee's expectations.

Independence

> All members of the Remuneration Committee should meet the test of independence.

Higgs Guidance

Independence is a cornerstone of the Remuneration Committee's effectiveness, particularly when determining appropriate levels of pay, and on any other issues where judgements and decisions are significant. Remuneration Committee members should be adept at communicating with management and should be ready to ask probing questions about the company's position and strategy, thus enabling them to determine the right level of stretch within the performance targets.

It is up to the board to assess the integrity and independence of a Remuneration Committee candidate; every member's appointment is an occasion for careful deliberation. The board should have a strong understanding of the relevant definitions of independence and should be aware of how a lack of independence might occur and be interpreted in practice. Issues of independence frequently occur in connection with business relations. The board should also be cognisant and mindful of situations in which the definition of independence is met, and yet perceived conflicts of interest can still arise.

The Combined Code states that the board should determine whether a director is independent in character and judgement and whether there are relationships or circumstances which are likely to affect, or could appear to affect, their judgement. Such relationships and circumstances include if the director:

- has been an employee of the company or group within the last five years;
- has, or has had within the last three years, a material business relationship with the company either directly, or as a partner, shareholder, director or senior employee of a body that has such a relationship with the company;
- has received or receives additional remuneration from the company other than a director's fee, participates in the company's share option or a performance-related pay scheme, or is a member of the company's pension scheme;
- has close family ties with any of the company's advisers, directors or senior employees;
- holds cross-directorships or has significant links with other directors through involvement in other companies or bodies;
- represents a significant shareholder; or
- has served on the board for more than nine years from the date of their first election.

Compliance with the revised Combined Code requires that Remuneration Committees should comprise at least three independent non-executive directors (two for companies outside the FTSE 350). For the avoidance of doubt, the Combined Code does not consider a board chairman to be independent in this context.[1]

There is an increasing requirement for non-executive directors to demonstrate that they are truly independent, to dispel the perceptions of the general public, the media and some shareholders that companies are run by a cushy network of 'old boys'. Additional pressure has been applied by the revisions of the Combined Code which require that at least half the board, excluding the chairman, comprise of independent non-executives. While this requirement immediately gave rise to concerns about the potential difficulties faced by companies in recruiting the requisite independent non-executive directors, this has not been borne out in practice. Some 84 per cent of the FTSE 100, and 58 per cent of the FTSE 250, comply with this provision.[2]

The National Association of Pension Funds (NAPF), an association that represents pension fund managers and trustees, has stated that concerns about the independence of Remuneration Committees will be dealt with differently, depending on what gave rise to the concern. Where previously they

1 The Combined Code will be amended in 2006 to allow the board chairman to sit on the remuneration committee, provided that he or she was independent on appointment.
2 KPMG's Directors' Compensation Survey 2005.

would recommend voting against the Remuneration Report if an executive or non-independent non-executive director sat on the Committee, in the case of the non-executive, they will now recommend a vote against the particular individual. Additionally they will oppose Remuneration Reports of companies which have not set up a Remuneration Committee. See Appendix 3 for NAPF's corporate governance policy, and Appendix 4 for their Contracts Best Practice document.

Skills and experience

Non-executive directors should constantly seek to establish and maintain confidence in the conduct of the company. They should be independent in judgement and have an enquiring mind. To be effective, non-executive directors need to build a recognition by executives of their contribution in order to promote openness and trust.

Higgs Guidance

Higgs believed that in order to be effective, all non-executive directors should:
- uphold the highest ethical standards of integrity and probity;
- support executives in their leadership of the business while monitoring their conduct;
- question intelligently, debate constructively, challenge rigorously and decide dispassionately;
- listen sensitively to the views of others, inside and outside the board;
- gain the trust and respect of other board members; and
- promote the highest standards of corporate governance and seek compliance with the provisions with the Combined Code wherever possible.

Remuneration Committee members will also need to possess background knowledge and skills with regard to remuneration. These could include:
- statistics to interpret market data;
- business acumen regarding performance measures;
- financial knowledge to understand option valuation and risk;
- pensions and actuarial knowledge;
- trust law;
- employment law;
- personal and company tax knowledge relating to remuneration issues.

A working knowledge of the above should help ensure that the non-executive director can participate fully in the work of the Remuneration Committee.

Remuneration Committee remuneration

The Combined Code states that the remuneration of non-executive directors should reflect their time commitment and responsibilities. The time commitment of non-executive directors may see a increase significantly, not only in terms of the number of meetings to attend, but also in terms of preparing for meetings, keeping abreast with company information and external changes, receiving formal training and development and communicating with shareholders. It was widely expected that the combination of the above, coupled with the threat of litigation and increased reputational risk, would mean that non-executive directors' fees would grow significantly. Indeed the median fee increase at those companies in the FTSE 100 that increased their fee levels in 2005 was 12 per cent.[3]

The RCI anticipates companies moving from providing an overall fee to a more structured fee composition, in line with the US, e.g. separate retainer fees, chairmanship fees, membership fees and attendance fees.

Remuneration Committee resources

The Remuneration Committee should be provided with sufficient resources to undertake its duties. It should have access to the services of the company secretary on all Remuneration Committee matters, including: assisting the chairman in planning the Remuneration Committee's work, drawing up meeting agendas, maintenance of minutes, drafting of material about its activities for the annual report, collection and distribution of information, and provision of any necessary practical support. The company secretary should aim to ensure that the Remuneration Committee receives information and papers in a timely manner to enable full and proper consideration to be given to the issues.

External consultants

The board should make funds available to the Remuneration Committee to enable it to take independent advice when the Remuneration Committee reasonably believes it necessary to do so.

At times the Remuneration Committee may require additional expertise to fulfil its role to a sufficiently high standard. External consultants can be used

3 KPMG's Directors' Compensation Survey 2005.

to provide market data, commentary on trends, help design incentive packages, and for benchmarking, best practice and tax and accounting advice. It is vital that the Remuneration Committee appoints external consultants on its own recommendation and that the consultants are independent of the company. The Enron scandal is one example of the conflict of interest that can arise when consultants are not independent. To help ensure that transparency and accountability to shareholders regarding directors' remuneration is maintained, external consultants must not be dependent on the executive for fees.

Professional development

All directors should receive induction on joining the board and should regularly update and refresh their skills and knowledge.

Combined Code Principle A.5

In his report on the role and effectiveness of non-executive directors, Sir Derek Higgs suggests that the induction process should aim to build an understanding of the nature of the company, its business and the markets in which it operates; it should build a link with the company's people as well as building an understanding of the company's main relationships. This can be achieved through presentations by senior management, site visits, specific training and mentoring.

Non-executive directors should be encouraged to continually update their skills. They should receive periodic continuing professional education both inside and outside of the boardroom. Management and the company secretary are sources of background information and training for audit committee members. Periodic briefings, reports and presentations by management, the HR director and external consultants should cover operational and executive compensation issues specific to the company and the industry.

3 Running an effective Remuneration Committee

This chapter looks at the practices that, based on our experience, mark a strong and effective Remuneration Committee, from its terms of reference through to monitoring the committee's performance.

Remuneration Committee terms of reference

In essence, the focus of the Remuneration Committee's terms of reference should define the scope of the committee's responsibilities and how these are to be discharged. The terms of reference should clearly outline the committee's duties and responsibilities, including structure, process and membership requirements.

In Appendix 5 we have included a guidance note issued by the Institute of Chartered Secretaries and Administrators (ICSA). This outlines Remuneration Committee terms of reference and will assist committees in creating or updating their complete terms of references consistent with Combined Code recommendations.

> The Remuneration Committee should make available its terms of reference, explaining its role and the authority delegated to it by the board.

Combined Code Provision B.2.1

A Remuneration Committee's terms of reference and responsibilities should be coordinated with other committee responsibilities. Care should be taken to define clearly the roles and responsibilities of each. Terms of reference should be detailed enough to clarify roles and responsibilities, but not so detailed that they include items that cannot be reasonably accomplished. The terms of reference should serve as a guide in establishing the Remuneration Committee's work plan and meeting agendas. The work plan should specifically set out how the Remuneration Committee intends to fulfil each of its responsibilities as disclosed in the terms of reference. It is very important that the Remuneration Committee takes into consideration the responsibilities laid out in the terms of reference as each meeting's agenda is set, and that responsibilities are reviewed on at least an annual basis, and updated where necessary. This review could be incorporated into the Remuneration Committee's self-evaluation process.

The annual assessment of the committee's terms of reference should be a robust process reflecting changes to the company's circumstances and any new regulations that may impact upon the Remuneration Committee's responsibilities.

The revised Combined Code recommends that the Remuneration Committee's terms of reference be disclosed to shareholders through inclusion on the company's websites – an increasing number of companies now do this.

Remuneration Committee meetings

A detailed agenda is vital for keeping the committee focused. Effective agendas are set with input from the CEO, HR director and external consultants. The Remuneration Committee chairman, however, should maintain accountability for the agenda and not delegate it to management. The Remuneration Committee agenda for the year should ideally originate from a detailed work plan. In turn, the detailed work plan should originate from the terms of reference. Appendix 6 and the accompanying CD include an example of Remuneration Committee agenda topics that should be considered when developing detailed Remuneration Committee agendas for the year. The timing of when these issues should be addressed is also included.

The Code does not specify a number with regard to the frequency of meetings, nor does it say anything about their timing, which would indicate that Remuneration Committees ought to meet as often as is necessary to fulfil their roles (at least once a year). The Code does state, however, that the number of meetings will differ from company to company and that they should be held at times when attendance will be maximised. The number of meetings and the level of attendance by the Remuneration Committee members should be reported in the annual reports.

Although the Code states that no one other than the committee chairman and members are entitled to be present at Remuneration Committee meetings, others are allowed to attend at the invitation of the committee. The chief executive officer and the chairman of the board often attend meetings as they can provide valuable information on the performance of particular individuals and the risk of such individuals leaving the organisation. The human resources or compensation and benefits director may also be invited to attend and can often be key to providing the committee with the papers it requires to conduct its meetings efficiently.

Communication policies

The content, timing and manner in which information is released both internally and externally by the company require levels of accountability and approval that should be defined, documented and approved by the board. Communication policies should consider guidelines to help ensure communications are not selective. Such policies should also consider crisis communications and electronic communication risks and controls.

> The chairman of the board should ensure that the company maintains contact as required with its principal shareholders about remuneration in the same way as for other matters.

Combined Code Supporting Principle B.2

The Remuneration Committee should actively contribute to setting the policy which delegates responsibility for the on-going dialogue on remuneration with shareholders to the most appropriate person. This may well be the chairman of the Remuneration Committee, the senior non-executive director, or the chairman of the board himself.

Assessing Remuneration Committee effectiveness

Something that is likely to have a significant impact on boardroom dynamics is the requirement in the Combined Code that the Board undertake a formal evaluation of its own performance and that of its committees and individual directors, and to disclose in the annual reports and accounts how this performance evaluation has been undertaken. Ninety per cent of FTSE 100 companies undertook some form of boardroom evaluation over the 2004 financial year. This figure compares favourably with the FTSE 250 companies, of which only 80 per cent assessed the performance of their directors, committees and boards. Most organisations that had not yet undertaken an evaluation, however, indicated that they would do so during the 2005 financial year.[1]

The process adopted to assess performance needs to be thought through carefully; there can be no 'one size fits all' approach. However, for an appraisal process to work effectively, there are some fundamental elements that should be present:

- *Independent control and objectivity.* To be credible and accountable, board and director evaluation processes must be independent of executive influence. The chairman, supported by the independent directors, should originate and control the assessment, taking into considerations the views of the CEO. The option of using external consultants to assist with the design and implementation could have the added benefit of bringing objectivity to the process.
- *Positive.* If board evaluation is to be more than a box-ticking exercise, it should be designed to encourage colleagues to be candid and constructive in their evaluation of each other's performance as individual directors, as well as their collective performance as a board.
- *Tailoring evaluations to the company and the board.* Boards should establish a process, including procedures and performance criteria, that suits the individuals and the company concerned.
- *Ensuring confidentiality and trust.* Boards should encourage openness, fairness and discretion in the evaluation process, while ensuring it maintains strict confidentiality with respect to each participant's input and feedback.
- *Regular review of the evaluation process.* Boards should periodically review assessment practices and criteria to measure their effectiveness and responsiveness against changing needs, and to help ensure continuing efficiency and appropriateness.
- *Feedback.* To help ensure credibility, it is important that those involved in the evaluation process receive constructive feedback.

Each year, the board should review the Remuneration Committee's effectiveness. In addition, the Remuneration Committee should assess its own effectiveness and the adequacy of its terms of reference, work plans, and forum of discussion and communication. This can be achieved by:

- questioning the board about its satisfaction with the committee's performance;

1 KPMG's Directors' Compensation Survey 2005.

- comparing the committee's activities to the recommendations of the Combined Code and the guidelines of the relevant securities exchanges;
- comparing the committee's activities to leading practices;
- comparing the committee's activities to the terms of reference and any other objectives the board set for the committee; and
- consulting with external advisors on ways to improve the Remuneration Committee's performance.

Each of these steps need not necessarily be performed annually, but all steps should be performed every two to three years. Any necessary changes should be recommended to the board.

The chairman of the Remuneration Committee should assess the performance of individual committee members on an annual basis. The Remuneration Committee in conjunction with the board should develop a formal and rigorous assessment process. This process may include interviews with the member being assessed, self-assessment and the assessment of members against standard criteria.

What marks a member who is successful? Someone who is dedicated to the committee's work and responsibilities; someone who is willing to devote the time necessary to understand the company and prepare for, attend and participate in meetings and deliberations; someone with an inquiring attitude, objectivity, independence and sound judgement.

The result of this assessment should be a recommendation to the board as to whether the member should be appointed for an additional term. The performance of the chairman would be evaluated by the board based upon similar criteria. Evaluations that are well performed demonstrate the committee's intention and commitment to fulfil its responsibilities in an effective and diligent manner.

An example self-assessment checklist is shown in Appendix 7 and is included on the accompanying CD.

4 Remuneration Committee responsibilities

The Remuneration Committee has a key role to play in the area of corporate governance. From Cadbury to Higgs, all have, to varying degrees, focused their attention on executive compensation and the ensuing responsibilities of the Remuneration Committee.

- **The Cadbury Report.**[1] Cadbury reduced the maximum contract length from five years to three; required full and clear disclosure of directors' total compensation, including pension contributions and stock options; and recommended that remuneration committees be made up wholly or mainly of non-executive directors.

- **The Greenbury Report.**[2] Sir Richard Greenbury set out three fundamental principles of executive remuneration: accountability, transparency and performance linkage. He also developed a code which has on the whole been subsumed by the revised Combined Code.

- **The Hampel Report.**[3] This report set out three main principles: the level and make up of remuneration; procedure and disclosure. These were incorporated into the Combined Code.

- **The Department of Trade and Industry's (DTI) consultation on directors' remuneration.** This consultation concluded that remuneration was an issue to be dealt with by shareholders and that the legal framework could be improved to aid their involvement. Many of these recommendations were included in the Directors' Remuneration Report Regulations 2002 (SI 2002/1986). These require increased and improved disclosure of remuneration and how it links to performance,

1 Sir Adrian Cadbury, *Report on the Financial Aspects of Corporate Governance*, 1992.
2 Sir Richard Greenbury, *Directors' Remuneration*, 1995.
3 Committee on Corporate Governance – Final Report Chaired by Sir Ronald Hampel, 1998.

and a vote at the AGM on the Remuneration Report. (For guidance on disclosure please see Appendix 8.)

- **The Higgs Report.**[4] As well as recommending that only independent directors should sit on the Remuneration Committee, which excluded the board chairman, Higgs set out a summary of the Remuneration Committee's principal duties, as follows:

> - determine and agree with the board the framework or broad policy for the remuneration of the chief executive, the chairman of the company and such other members of the executive management as it is designated to consider*. At a minimum, the committee should have delegated responsibility for setting remuneration for all executive directors, the chairman and, to maintain and assure their independence, the company secretary. The remuneration of non-executive directors should be a matter for the chairman and executive members of the board. No director or manager should be involved in any decisions as to their own remuneration;
> - determine targets for any performance-related pay schemes operated by the company;
> - determine the policy for and scope of pension arrangements for each executive director;
> - ensure that contractual terms on termination, and any payments made, are fair to the individual and the company, that failure is not rewarded and that the duty to mitigate loss is fully recognised;**
> - within the terms of the agreed policy, determine the total individual remuneration package of each executive director including, where appropriate, bonuses, incentive payments and share options;
> - in determining such packages and arrangements, give due regard to the comments and recommendations of the Code as well as the UK Listing Authority's Listing Rules and associated guidance;
> - be aware of and advise on any major changes in employee benefit structures throughout the company or group;
> - agree the policy for authorising claims for expenses from the chief executive and chairman;

4 Derek Higgs, *Review of the Role and Effectiveness of Non-executive Directors*, 2003.

- ensure that provisions regarding disclosure of remuneration, including pensions, as set out in the Directors' Remuneration Report Regulations 2002 and the Code, are fulfilled;
- be exclusively responsible for establishing the selection criteria, selecting, appointing and setting the terms of reference for any remuneration consultants who advise the committee;
- report the frequency of, and attendance by members at, Remuneration Committee meetings in the annual report; and
- make the committee's terms of reference publicly available. These should set out the committee's delegated responsibilities and be reviewed and, where necessary, updated annually.

* Some companies require the Remuneration Committee to consider the packages of all executives at or above a specified level such as those reporting to a main board director whilst other require the committee to deal with all packages above a certain figure.

** Remuneration Committees should consider reviewing and agreeing a standard form of contract for its executive directors, and try to ensure that new appointees are offered and accept terms within the previously agreed level.

Setting remuneration for directors and senior executives

In today's market, institutional investors pay very close attention to remuneration levels and are only prepared to accept increases that go hand in hand with more stringent performance targets. From their point of view, base salaries should be set at around the median, and the same applies to annual bonuses. Any changes to overall levels therefore should be made through the longer-term performance-related elements of remuneration, with the net result being that over time, executive packages are likely to become increasingly geared to the company's performance and achieve a greater alignment with the interests of shareholders.

The performance-related elements of remuneration should form a significant proportion of the total remuneration package of executive directors and should be designed to align their interests with those of shareholders.

Combined Code Provision B.1.1

To reassure shareholders that the right balance is being reached, much emphasis is placed upon the policy-setting procedure being formal and transparent, and it stands to reason that any executive involvement should be strictly at arm's-length, and that it is the Remuneration Committee that has responsibility for appointing the remuneration consultants and advisers. In turn, the chairman of the board must ensure that shareholders are apprised of remuneration issues in the same way that they would be informed of any other corporate issue.

> There should be a formal and transparent procedure for developing policy on executive remuneration.

Combined Code Principle B.2

Reviewing the appropriateness of the remuneration framework and policy

One of the Remuneration Committee's key tasks is to offer levels of remuneration which satisfy the simultaneous requirements of attracting, retaining and motivating the very people who are vital to the company's success. In doing so, the balance to be sought is that they avoid paying more than is necessary to fulfil that task.

Monitoring the company's incentivisation arrangements is an on-going process in which the Remuneration Committee should determine their effectiveness with regard to the main requirement of recruitment, retention and motivation.

The committee should be satisfied that overall packages are well positioned relative to those of other companies. In some cases a company's remuneration policy vis-à-vis those of other companies could be all too apparent where there are staff losses, but by then, arguably, it may be a pointless exercise. The preferable alternative is to set about an objective benchmarking exercise which should enable the Remuneration Committee to make adjustments to executive packages that pre-empt unwanted departures. Appendix 9 and the accompanying CD set out an overview of a methodology for a benchmarking process.

Determining the appropriate performance targets and suitable levels of stringency will require a fine understanding of the company's strategic position and prospects as well as the key value drivers within that business.

Payouts or grants under all incentive schemes, including new grants under existing option schemes, should be subject to challenging performance criteria reflecting the company's objectives.

Combined Code Schedule A

In addition the Remuneration Committee should be aware of the expectations of the shareholders in this regard and may well want the flexibility to hold back awards unless the underlying financial performance of the company warrants their vesting.

Issues for Remuneration Committees to consider when designing incentive schemes

IFRS 2 accounting for share-based payments

Perhaps the most significant impact on remuneration strategies of IFRS 2 and its UK equivalent, FRS 20, has been to cause companies to reassess whether their incumbent remuneration arrangements offer value for money. There will be considerable interest in the accounting costs of all long-term incentive plans and thus a consideration as to whether current, and any new plans, offer 'value for money.'

In addition, shareholders are likely to be paying close attention to consistent measures of performance as a result of the transition to international accounting standards. The ABI, in their revised guidelines published in December 2005, state that 'during the transition to international accounting standards, shareholders expect Remuneration Committees to confirm that they are using a consistent approach to performance measurement and to explain how they are achieving this.'

The pensions tax simplification rules – lifetime allowance

The pensions tax simplification rules – the lifetime allowance of £1.5m, which took effect in April 2006 – will impact a significant number of FTSE 350 executive directors as well as a sizeable population of executives below the board. While it is clearly recognised that the new regime will have a significant impact, it will take some time to assess the full impact on total compensation.

Quantum

While increases in executive salary have been less than in recent years, institutional investors are growing increasingly concerned about the trend to increase the total remuneration package through higher incentive plan awards and the granting of awards under multiple plans. The question on a few shareholders' lips is 'How much is too much?'

The reference to remuneration being set in the context of the business size, complexity and geographical location has been removed and the revised ABI guidelines now stress that 'external comparisons should be used with caution, in view of an upward ratchet of remuneration levels with no corresponding improvement in performance and [businesses] should avoid paying more than is necessary.' It is still unclear what the practical outcome of this change will be.

Shareholders are also likely to pay close attention to the possibility of unjustified windfall gains. Companies are being urged to ensure that performance measurements governing variable and share-based remuneration are robust, that Remuneration Committees satisfy themselves as to the accuracy of recorded performance measures that govern testing, and that audit committees are involved in evaluating performance criteria.

Retesting of performance criteria

Shareholder pressure to remove retesting from long-term incentives continues. Part of the shareholders' argument is that many long-term incentives are now granted on an annual basis and therefore, if the performance conditions have not been met at the end of three years, the executive is still sitting on two outstanding awards which should incentivise them. Whether or not companies agree with this, the vast majority of new long-term incentive plans do not have retesting in respect of awards made to directors. Furthermore, a number of companies have removed retesting from existing plans.

The NAPF's latest position is to recommend a vote against the Remuneration Report of any company which has not removed retesting from existing incentive schemes.

Disclosure of annual bonus arrangements

Under the revised ABI guidelines there is a new expectation to provide more details of the extent to which prior year annual targets have been met. By requiring only backward-looking disclosures on targets, the ABI is addressing companies' concerns that some data relating to annual bonus performance targets may be commercially sensitive. In addition, the new guidelines include a requirement that any increases in the maximum bonus potential from one year to the next should be explicitly justified.

Portfolio diversification

The NAPF has identified some cases where companies have allowed the beneficiaries of long-term incentive schemes to exchange their vesting shares in the company for a diversified portfolio of shares. The NAPF is concerned that the cost of such an exercise is borne by the company and its shareholders, and not by the individual concerned. In addition, this does not support the NAPF's wish to see executives building up meaningful investments in their employers. The NAPF will look at such arrangements on a case-by-case basis, but may recommend a vote against the Remuneration Report if the explanation for such an arrangement is unclear. This was a new issue for 2005, and companies considering such arrangements should take note of the NAPF's stance.

The American Jobs Creation Act of 2004 (the JCA)

Key changes to the provisions on deferred compensation mean that, in general, for deferrals after 31 December 2004, the tax point for many deferral arrangements moves forward from the time when the award is exercised/distributed to the vesting date, and the participant may be subject to a 20 per cent additional tax charge and an interest penalty. Many awards under the types of plan listed below will be caught by the JCA provisions, resulting in additional tax charges for employees. Companies should consider introducing new arrangements if their existing plans are caught by the new law or are no longer commercially appropriate.

Although fair value stock options are excluded, deferral arrangements affected include:

- international SAYE plans under which awards are made (at a discount) to US participants;
- stock appreciation rights and phantom share plans (many of which are adopted because of securities laws in certain states (e.g. California));
- elective bonus deferral/bonus match plans, deferred share plans and other long-term incentive plans where there is a delay between vesting of awards and distribution of proceeds;
- plans which provide for accelerated vesting other than as permitted specifically by regulation.

To meet the JCA requirements and avoid the accelerated tax charge, plans must only allow distributions in certain circumstances (i.e. cessation of employment, disability, death or an otherwise pre-specified time) and only permit accelerated vesting in limited circumstances. Elections to defer salary-based compensation must (broadly) be entered into before the start of the calendar year in which the compensation would be earned.

Share ownership

Institutional investors believe that executive directors should be encouraged to build up shareholdings in their company. By and large they are happy to encourage non-executive directors to do the same, although they would be wary of holdings so significant that they impair their independence.

Change of control

The revised ABI guidelines indicate a further tightening in the views of institutional investors on the issue of the early vesting of share incentives in the event of a change of control. In particular, the ABI will look to Remuneration Committees to consider how they will apply the principle of pro rating of share awards vesting, taking account of the amount of the vesting period that had elapsed at the time of the change in control, if and when necessary in terms of making allowance for any reduction in value resulting from truncation of the life of an option, and to provide a clear explanation of their position to shareholders. The requirement for no automatic waiver of performance conditions in the event of a change in control remains the same.

The guidelines also ask that 'Remuneration Committees should use best endeavours to provide meaningful disclosure that quantifies the aggregate payments arising on a change of control'.[5] In addition, it is stated for the first time that 'Remuneration Committees should satisfy themselves that the performance criterion genuinely reflects a robust measure of underlying financial achievement over any shorter time period [and that] they should explain their reasoning in the remuneration report or other relevant documentation sent to shareholders'.[6]

Clearly this issue is moving up the list of areas of concern for institutional investors. It is worth nothing that both the NAPF (2004) and the PIRC (2005)

5 Association of British Insurers, 'Principles and Guidelines on Remuneration,' December 2005
6 Ibid.

voting guidelines require the vesting of awards to take account of the extent to which performance conditions have been met and to pro-rate for the time elapsed since grant.

The indications are that many companies in the FTSE 100 and the wider index have adopted the earlier guidelines on change of control.

The newly stated requirement that committees should satisfy themselves that the performance measurement genuinely reflects a robust measure of underlying financial achievement over any shorter time period indicates that institutional investors are likely to expect performance conditions to capture underlying financial performance as well as the share price growth where measurements such as TSR are adopted.

EU Prospectus Directive

The provisions of this Directive will be incorporated into UK law and became effective from 1 July 2005. The intention is to introduce a single EU regime for the content, approval and publication of prospectuses in the EU.

From 1 July 2005, all awards under director and employee share plans (such as share options, performance and LTIPs) will need to comply with the Directive (whether granted under a new or existing plan). In particular the company issuing the awards will need to be comfortable that one of the exemptions is available (including complying with any conditions for the exemption to apply) or publish a prospectus complaint with the Directive.

There are a number of exemptions that allow awards to be made without publishing a full prospectus. However, many of these exemptions are less generous than exemptions already in existence under UK law, and a number have conditions which need to be complied with for the exemption to be available.

Companies making offers in more than one country should beware, as some countries may not have incorporated the directive into their domestic law with effect from 1 July 2005. The requirements in each country will therefore need to be ascertained before offers are made.

Internal pay comparisons

There will be times when the Remuneration Committee will need to be able to communicate compensation arrangements sensitively. At times, trade unions and employees have difficulty in understanding why they are restricted to, for instance, a 3 per cent salary increase while executives enjoy a 7 per cent increase. The NAPF guidelines state that it is now 'Good Practice for Boards to disclose in their annual report, the average total annual remuneration of executive directors and the average total annual remuneration of non-Board employees in the financial year'. They also expect companies to adopt a policy with respect to the ratio between these amounts, and to publish the ratio both for the current and the prior year. This may seem a debatable statistic but the internal comparison is in sharp focus for many. Companies should at least aim to ensure clear communication.

Combined Code

Recent times have been far from dull, to say the least, for non-executive directors. The spate of scandals in the US of Enron and WorldCom, which have now become textbook cases, and, closer to home those of Ahold, Equitable Life and Parmalat, means that the pressure on non-executive directors is not relenting. Moreover, the new disclosure requirements, not only on executive remuneration, but also on the board processes, are increasing the scrutiny on the operation of the board. Institutional shareholders now expect more communication and consultation between non-executive directors and themselves. As shareholders also focus on areas of non-compliance with the Combined Code, but with modest resources, we anticipate a movement from the current 'comply or explain' environment to more of a 'comply and comply' one.

That said, shareholders continue to support the principle of 'comply or explain' by basing their position in the updated guidelines on exercising judgement and on being pragmatic when needed, for example in interpreting the 'nine-year rule' for determining the independence of non-executive directors.

Performance evaluation and the role of the Remuneration Committee

In determining levels of executive remuneration the Remuneration Committee should look at the wider picture. As discussed previously, the revised Combined Code now requires boards to evaluate their own performance, that of their committees and individual directors on an annual basis.

Non-executive director evaluation is relatively straightforward. The board, led by the chairman, must assess whether the non-executive director continues to contribute effectively and to demonstrate commitment to the role (including commitment of time for board and committee meetings and any other duties). The chairman should discuss performance with the individual concerned and if appropriate seek either to develop the skills of the individual or, in extraordinary circumstances, request the resignation of an under-performing director.

However, the case of the executive director is more complicated. On the one hand he should be assessed in exactly the same way as his non-executive counterpart in relation to his role as board member. On the other hand he will already be subject to operational targets and be evaluated against those targets by his CEO. This raises several issues. How will the CEO and the chairman co-ordinate their evaluations? How can this then link into the work of the Remuneration Committee, who will have views on how they link the performance to the director's pay?

The situation could be muddled further if the director's performance is inconsistent. For example, a sales director during the year may have performed against targets on an operational level but because he has been so dedicated to this role he rarely turns up at board meetings and when he does, he is ill-prepared. He is quite clearly a valuable asset to the organisation, in that he has generated a huge amount of revenue, but has not demonstrated much commitment to his role as board member and in turn has not contributed to its effectiveness. These are issues that need to be thought through carefully; there is no 'one size fits all' approach.

Appendices

The CD which accompanies this book reproduces Appendices 1–12 so that they can be easily adapted to suit individual requirements.

Appendix 1
Financial Reporting Council Combined Code on Corporate Governance

SECTION 1 COMPANIES

A. DIRECTORS

A.1 The Board

Main Principle

Every company should be headed by an effective board, which is collectively responsible for the success of the company.

Supporting Principles

The board's role is to provide entrepreneurial leadership of the company within a framework of prudent and effective controls which enables risk to be assessed and managed. The board should set the company's strategic aims, ensure that the necessary financial and human resources are in place for the company to meet its objectives and review management performance. The board should set the company's values and standards and ensure that its obligations to its shareholders and others are understood and met.

All directors must take decisions objectively in the interests of the company. As part of their role as members of a unitary board, non-executive directors should constructively challenge and help develop proposals on strategy. Non-executive directors should scrutinise the performance of management in meeting agreed goals and objectives and monitor the reporting of performance. They should satisfy themselves on the integrity of financial information and that financial controls and systems of risk management are robust and defensible. They are responsible for determining appropriate levels of remuneration of executive directors and have a prime role in appointing, and where necessary removing, executive directors, and in succession planning.

Code Provisions

A.1.1   The board should meet sufficiently regularly to discharge its duties effectively. There should be a formal schedule of matters specifically reserved for its decision. The annual report should include a statement of how the board operates, including a high level statement of which types of decisions are to be taken by the board and which are to be delegated to management.

A.1.2 The annual report should identify the chairman, the deputy chairman (where there is one), the chief executive, the senior independent director and the chairmen and members of the nomination, audit and remuneration committees. It should also set out the number of meetings of the board and those committees and individual attendance by directors.

A.1.3 The chairman should hold meetings with the non-executive directors without the executives present. Led by the senior independent director, the non-executive directors should meet without the chairman present at least annually to appraise the chairman's performance (as described in A.6.1) and on such other occasions as are deemed appropriate.

A.1.4 Where directors have concerns which cannot be resolved about the running of the company or a proposed action, they should ensure that their concerns are recorded in the board minutes. On resignation, a non-executive director should provide a written statement to the chairman, for circulation to the board, if they have any such concerns.

A.1.5 The company should arrange appropriate insurance cover in respect of legal action against its directors.

A.2 Chairman and chief executive

Main Principle

There should be a clear division of responsibilities at the head of the company between the running of the board and the executive responsibility for the running of the company's business. No one individual should have unfettered powers of decision.

Supporting Principle

The chairman is responsible for leadership of the board, ensuring its effectiveness on all aspects of its role and setting its agenda. The chairman is also responsible for ensuring that the directors receive accurate, timely and clear information. The chairman should ensure effective communication with shareholders. The chairman should also facilitate the effective contribution of non-executive directors in particular and ensure constructive relations between executive and non-executive directors.

Code Provisions

A.2.1 The roles of chairman and chief executive should not be exercised by the same individual. The division of responsibilities between the chairman and chief executive should be clearly established, set out in writing and agreed by the board.

A.2.2[1] The chairman should on appointment meet the independence criteria set out in A.3.1 below. A chief executive should not go on to be chairman of the same company. If exceptionally a board decides that a chief executive should become chairman, the board should consult major shareholders in advance and should set out its reasons to shareholders at the time of the appointment and in the next annual report.

A.3 Board balance and independence

Main Principle

The board should include a balance of executive and non-executive directors (and in particular independent non-executive directors) such that no individual or small group of individuals can dominate the board's decision taking.

Supporting Principles

The board should not be so large as to be unwieldy. The board should be of sufficient size that the balance of skills and experience is appropriate for the requirements of the business and that changes to the board's composition can be managed without undue disruption. To ensure that power and information are not concentrated in one or two individuals, there should be a strong presence on the board of both executive and non-executive directors.

The value of ensuring that committee membership is refreshed and that undue reliance is not placed on particular individuals should be taken into account in deciding chairmanship and membership of committees. No one other than the committee chairman and members is entitled to be present at a meeting of the nomination, audit or remuneration committee, but others may attend at the invitation of the committee.

---

1 (Combined Code footnote 5): compliance or otherwise with this provision need only be reported for the year in which the appointment is made.

Code provisions

A.3.1 The board should identify in the annual report each non-executive director it considers to be independent.[2] The board should determine whether the director is independent in character and judgement and whether there are relationships or circumstances which are likely to affect, or could appear to affect, the director's judgement. The board should state its reasons if it determines that a director is independent notwithstanding the existence of relationships or circumstances which may appear relevant to its determination, including if the director:

– has been an employee of the company or group within the last five years;

– has, or has had within the last three years, a material business relationship with the company either directly, or as a partner, shareholder, director or senior employee of a body that has such a relationship with the company;

– has received or receives additional remuneration from the company apart from a director's fee, participates in the company's share option or a performance-related pay scheme, or is a member of the company's pension scheme;

– has close family ties with any of the company's advisers, directors or senior employees;

– holds cross-directorships or has significant links with other directors through involvement in other companies or bodies;

– represents a significant shareholder; or

– has served on the board for more than nine years from the date of their first election.

A.3.2 Except for smaller companies,[3] at least half the board, excluding the chairman, should comprise non-executive directors determined by the board to be independent. A smaller company should have at least two independent non-executive directors.

A.3.3 The board should appoint one of the independent non-executive directors to be the senior independent director. The senior independent director should

---

2 (Combined Code footnote 6): A.2.2 states that the chairman should, on appointment, meet the independence criteria set out in this provision, but thereafter the test of independence is not appropriate in relation to the chairman.

3 (Combined Code footnote 7): a smaller company is one that is below the FTSE 350 throughout the year immediately prior to the reporting year.

be available to shareholders if they have concerns which contact through the normal channels of chairman, chief executive or finance director has failed to resolve or for which such contact is inappropriate.

A.4 Appointments to the Board

Main Principle

There should be a formal, rigorous and transparent procedure for the appointment of new directors to the board.

Supporting Principles

Appointments to the board should be made on merit and against objective criteria. Care should be taken to ensure that appointees have enough time available to devote to the job. This is particularly important in the case of chairmanships. The board should satisfy itself that plans are in place for orderly succession for appointments to the board and to senior management, so as to maintain an appropriate balance of skills and experience within the company and on the board.

Code Provisions

A.4.1   There should be a nomination committee which should lead the process for board appointments and make recommendations to the board. A majority of members of the nomination committee should be independent non-executive directors. The chairman or an independent non-executive director should chair the committee, but the chairman should not chair the nomination committee when it is dealing with the appointment of a successor to the chairmanship. The nomination committee should make available[4] its terms of reference, explaining its role and the authority delegated to it by the board.

A.4.2   The nomination committee should evaluate the balance of skills, knowledge and experience on the board and, in the light of this evaluation, prepare a description of the role and capabilities required for a particular appointment.

A.4.3   For the appointment of a chairman, the nomination committee should prepare a job specification, including an assessment of the time commitment expected, recognising the need for availability in the event of crises. A chairman's other significant commitments should be disclosed to the board

4 (Combined Code footnote 8): the requirement to make the information available would be met by making it available on request and by including the information on the company's website.

before appointment and included in the annual report. Changes to such commitments should be reported to the board as they arise, and included in the next annual report. No individual should be appointed to a second chairmanship of a FTSE 100 company.[5]

A.4.4 The terms and conditions of appointment of non-executive directors should be made available for inspection. The letter of appointment should set out the expected time commitment. Non-executive directors should undertake that they will have sufficient time to meet what is expected of them. Their other significant commitments should be disclosed to the board before appointment, with a broad indication of the time involved and the board should be informed of subsequent changes.

A.4.5 The board should not agree to a full-time executive director taking on more than one non-executive directorship in a FTSE 100 company nor the chairmanship of such a company.

A.4.6 A separate section of the annual report should describe the work of the nomination committee, including the process it has used in relation to board appointments. An explanation should be given if neither an external search consultancy nor open advertising has been used in the appointment of a chairman or a non-executive director.

A.5 Information and professional development

Main Principle

The board should be supplied in a timely manner with information in a form and of a quality appropriate to enable it to discharge its duties. All directors should receive induction on joining the board and should regularly update and refresh their skills and knowledge.

Supporting Principles

The chairman is responsible for ensuring that the directors receive accurate, timely and clear information. Management has an obligation to provide such information but directors should seek clarification or amplification where necessary. The chairman should ensure that the directors continually update their skills and the knowledge and familiarity with the company required to fulfil their role both on the board and on board committees. The company should provide the necessary resources for developing and updating its directors' knowledge and capabilities. Under the direc-

---

5 (Combined Code footnote 9): compliance or otherwise with this provision need only be reported for the year in which the appointment is made.

tion of the chairman, the company secretary's responsibilities include ensuring good information flows within the board and its committees and between senior management and non-executive directors, as well as facilitating induction and assisting with professional development as required. The company secretary should be responsible for advising the board through the chairman on all governance matters.

Code Provisions

A.5.1 The chairman should ensure that new directors receive a full, formal and tailored induction on joining the board. As part of this, the company should offer to major shareholders the opportunity to meet a new non-executive director.

A.5.2 The board should ensure that directors, especially non-executive directors, have access to independent professional advice at the company's expense where they judge it necessary to discharge their responsibilities as directors. Committees should be provided with sufficient resources to undertake their duties.

A.5.3 All directors should have access to the advice and services of the company secretary, who is responsible to the board for ensuring that board procedures are complied with. Both the appointment and removal of the company secretary should be a matter for the board as a whole.

A.6 Performance evaluation

Main Principle

The board should undertake a formal and rigorous annual evaluation of its own performance and that of its committees and individual directors.

Supporting Principle

Individual evaluation should aim to show whether each director continues to contribute effectively and to demonstrate commitment to the role (including commitment of time for board and committee meetings and any other duties). The chairman should act on the results of the performance evaluation by recognising the strengths and addressing the weaknesses of the board and, where appropriate, proposing new members be appointed to the board or seeking the resignation of directors.

Code Provision

A.6.1 The board should state in the annual report how performance evaluation of the board, its committees and its individual directors has been conducted. The non-executive directors, led by the senior independent director, should be responsible for performance evaluation of the chairman, taking into account the views of executive directors.

A.7 Re-election

Main Principle

All directors should be submitted for re-election at regular intervals, subject to continued satisfactory performance. The board should ensure planned and progressive refreshing of the board.

Code Provisions

A.7.1 All directors should be subject to election by shareholders at the first annual general meeting after their appointment, and to re-election thereafter at intervals of no more than three years. The names of directors submitted for election or re-election should be accompanied by sufficient biographical details and any other relevant information to enable shareholders to take an informed decision on their election.

A.7.2 Non-executive directors should be appointed for specified terms subject to re-election and to Companies Acts provisions relating to the removal of a director. The board should set out to shareholders in the papers accompanying a resolution to elect a non-executive director why they believe an individual should be elected. The chairman should confirm to shareholders when proposing re-election that, following formal performance evaluation, the individual's performance continues to be effective and to demonstrate commitment to the role. Any term beyond six years (e.g. two three-year terms) for a non-executive director should be subject to particularly rigorous review, and should take into account the need for progressive refreshing of the board. Non-executive directors may serve longer than nine years (e.g. three three-year terms), subject to annual re-election. Serving more than nine years could be relevant to the determination of a non-executive director's independence (as set out in provision A.3.1).

B. REMUNERATION

B.1 The Level and Make-up of Remuneration

Main Principle

Levels of remuneration should be sufficient to attract, retain and motivate directors of the quality required to run the company successfully, but a company should avoid

paying more than is necessary for this purpose. A significant proportion of executive directors' remuneration should be structured so as to link rewards to corporate and individual performance.

Supporting Principle

The remuneration committee should judge where to position their company relative to other companies. But they should use such comparisons with caution, in view of the risk of an upward ratchet of remuneration levels with no corresponding improvement in performance. They should also be sensitive to pay and employment conditions elsewhere in the group, especially when determining annual salary increases.

Code Provisions

Remuneration policy

B.1.1   The performance-related elements of remuneration should form a significant proportion of the total remuneration package of executive directors and should be designed to align their interests with those of shareholders and to give these directors keen incentives to perform at the highest levels. In designing schemes of performance-related remuneration, the remuneration committee should follow the provisions in Schedule A to this Code.

B.1.2   Executive share options should not be offered at a discount save as permitted by the relevant provisions of the Listing Rules.

B.1.3   Levels of remuneration for non-executive directors should reflect the time commitment and responsibilities of the role. Remuneration for non-executive directors should not include share options. If, exceptionally, options are granted, shareholder approval should be sought in advance and any shares acquired by exercise of the options should be held until at least one year after the non-executive director leaves the board. Holding of share options could be relevant to the determination of a non-executive director's independence (as set out in provision A.3.1).

B.1.4   Where a company releases an executive director to serve as a non-executive director elsewhere, the remuneration report[6] should include a statement as to whether or not the director will retain such earnings and, if so, what the remuneration is.

---

6 (Combined Code footnote 12): as required under the Directors' Remuneration Report Regulations.

Service Contracts and Compensation

B.1.5   The remuneration committee should carefully consider what compensation commitments (including pension contributions and all other elements) their directors' terms of appointment would entail in the event of early termination. The aim should be to avoid rewarding poor performance. They should take a robust line on reducing compensation to reflect departing directors' obligations to mitigate loss.

B.1.6   Notice or contract periods should be set at one year or less. If it is necessary to offer longer notice or contract periods to new directors recruited from outside, such periods should reduce to one year or less after the initial period.

B.2 Procedure

Main Principle

There should be a formal and transparent procedure for developing policy on executive remuneration and for fixing the remuneration packages of individual directors. No director should be involved in deciding his or her own remuneration.

Supporting Principles

The remuneration committee should consult the chairman and/or chief executive about their proposals relating to the remuneration of other executive directors. The remuneration committee should also be responsible for appointing any consultants in respect of executive director remuneration. Where executive directors or senior management are involved in advising or supporting the remuneration committee, care should be taken to recognise and avoid conflicts of interest. The chairman of the board should ensure that the company maintains contact as required with its principal shareholders about remuneration in the same way as for other matters.

Code Provisions

B.2.1   The board should establish a remuneration committee of at least three, or in the case of smaller companies, two members, who should all be independent non-executive directors. The remuneration committee should make available its terms of reference, explaining its role and the authority delegated to it by the board. Where remuneration consultants are appointed, a statement should be made available of whether they have any other connection with the company.

B.2.2   The remuneration committee should have delegated responsibility for setting remuneration for all executive directors and the chairman, including pension rights and any compensation payments. The committee should also recommend and monitor the level and structure of remuneration for senior management. The definition of 'senior management' for this purpose should be determined by the board but should normally include the first layer of management below board level.

B.2.3   The board itself or, where required by the Articles of Association, the shareholders should determine the remuneration of the non-executive directors within the limits set in the Articles of Association. Where permitted by the Articles, the board may however delegate this responsibility to a committee, which might include the chief executive.

B.2.4   Shareholders should be invited specifically to approve all new long-term incentive schemes (as defined in the Listing Rules) and significant changes to existing schemes, save in the circumstances permitted by the Listing Rules.

D. RELATIONS WITH SHAREHOLDERS

D.1 Dialogue with Institutional Shareholders

Main Principle

There should be a dialogue with shareholders based on the mutual understanding of objectives. The board as a whole has responsibility for ensuring that a satisfactory dialogue with shareholders takes place.

Supporting Principles

Whilst recognising that most shareholder contact is with the chief executive and finance director, the chairman (and the senior independent director and other directors as appropriate) should maintain sufficient contact with major shareholders to understand their issues and concerns. The board should keep in touch with shareholder opinion in whatever ways are most practical and efficient.

Code Provisions

D.1.1   The chairman should ensure that the views of shareholders are communicated to the board as a whole. The chairman should discuss governance and strategy with major shareholders. Non-executive directors should be offered the opportunity to attend meetings with major shareholders and should expect to attend them if requested by major shareholders. The senior independent director should attend sufficient meetings with a range of major shareholders to listen to their views in order to help develop a balanced understanding of the issues and concerns of major shareholders.

D.1.2   The board should state in the annual report the steps they have taken to ensure that the members of the board, and in particular the non-executive directors, develop an understanding of the views of major shareholders about their company, for example through direct face-to-face contact, analysts' or brokers' briefings and surveys of shareholder opinion.

D.2 Constructive Use of the AGM

Main Principle

The board should use the AGM to communicate with investors and to encourage their participation.

Code Provisions

D.2.1   The company should count all proxy votes and, except where a poll is called, should indicate the level of proxies lodged on each resolution, and the balance for and against the resolution and the number of abstentions, after it has been dealt with on a show of hands. The company should ensure that votes cast are properly received and recorded.

D.2.2   The company should propose a separate resolution at the AGM on each substantially separate issue and should in particular propose a resolution at the AGM relating to the report and accounts.

D.2.3   The chairman should arrange for the chairmen of the audit, remuneration and nomination committees to be available to answer questions at the AGM and for all directors to attend.

D.2.4   The company should arrange for the Notice of the AGM and related papers to be sent to shareholders at least 20 working days before the meeting.

SECTION 2 INSTITUTIONAL SHAREHOLDERS

E. INSTITUTIONAL SHAREHOLDERS[7]

E.1 Dialogue with companies

Main Principle

Institutional shareholders should enter into a dialogue with companies based on the mutual understanding of objectives.

Supporting Principles

Institutional shareholders should apply the principles set out in the Institutional Shareholders' Committee's 'The Responsibilities of Institutional Shareholders and Agents – Statement of Principles'[8] which should be reflected in fund manager contracts.

E.2 Evaluation of Governance Disclosures

Main Principle

When evaluating companies' governance arrangements, particularly those relating to board structure and composition, institutional shareholders should give due weight to all relevant factors drawn to their attention.

Supporting Principle

Institutional shareholders should consider carefully explanations given for departure from this Code and make reasoned judgements in each case. They should give an explanation to the company, in writing where appropriate, and be prepared to enter a dialogue if they do not accept the company's position. They should avoid a box-ticking approach to assessing a company's corporate governance. In particular, they should bear in mind the size and complexity of the company and the nature of the risks and challenges it faces.

7 (Combined Code footnote 21): agents such as investment managers, or voting services, are frequently appointed by institutional shareholders to act on their behalf and these principles should accordingly be read as applying where appropriate to the agents of institutional shareholders.

8 (Combined Code footnote 22): available at website www.investmentuk.org.uk.

E.3 Shareholder Voting

Main Principle

Institutional shareholders have a responsibility to make considered use of their votes.

Supporting Principles

Institutional shareholders should take steps to ensure their voting intentions are being translated into practice. Institutional shareholders should, on request, make available to their clients information on the proportion of resolutions on which votes were cast and non-discretionary proxies lodged. Major shareholders should attend AGMs where appropriate and practicable. Companies and registrars should facilitate this.

Appendix 2
Directors' Remuneration Report Regulations (Schedule 7A)

The following are extracts from the Directors' Remuneration Report Regulations that are relevant to remuneration committee members.

The Directors' Remuneration Report Regulations that came into effect as of August 2002 require that a resolution approving the directors' remuneration report be put before shareholders at the general meeting of the company. Part 2 of Schedule 7A requires information concerning four areas:

- circumstances surrounding the consideration by the directors of matters pertaining to directors' remuneration;

- a statement of the company's policy on directors' remuneration for the following financial year;

- a performance graph which sets out the total shareholder return of the company on the class of equity share capital, if any, which caused the company to fall within the definition of 'quoted company';

- certain information to be set out concerning each director's contract of service or contract for services.

Part 3 of Schedule 7A requires detailed information to be set out concerning the emoluments, share options, long-term incentive plans, pensions, compensation and excess retirement benefits of each director and, in some cases, of past directors as well. The accompanying checklist will enable the Remuneration Committee to ensure that the Remuneration Report is compliant with the legal requirements.

Source: Directors' Remuneration Report Regulations (Schedule 7A)	Company X	
	Reference	Checklist
PART 2 – INFORMATION NOT SUBJECT TO AUDIT		
2 Consideration by the directors of matters relating to directors remuneration		
Consideration by the directors of matters relating to directors' remuneration	Part 2 para 2(1)	
Names of directors who were members of the Remuneration Committee (or any other committee who has considered directors' remuneration matters during the financial year (FY))	Part 2 para 2(1)(a)	
Names of persons who provided advice/services (and nature of other services provided and whether appointed by the Committee if they were not directors) that materially assisted the Committee	Part 2 para 2(1)(b), (c)	
3 Statement of policy on directors' remuneration		
Statement of policy on directors' remuneration for the following financial year and subsequent years	Part 2 para 3(1)	
For each director, a detailed summary of performance conditions of share options and LTIP awards	Part 2 para 3(2)(a)	
An explanation of why such performance conditions were chosen	Part 2 para 3(2)(b)	
A summary of methods used (and rationale for using them) in assessing whether performance measures are met	Part 2 para 3(2)(c)	
A summary of factors used in making each comparison and where any of the factors relate to the performance of other companies or an index on which the shares of those companies are listed, the identity of each company or of the index	Part 2 para 3(2)(d)	

Source: Directors' Remuneration Report Regulations (Schedule 7A)	Company X	
	Reference	Checklist
A description of and explanation for any significant amendment proposed to be made to the terms and conditions of any entitlement of a director to share options or LTIP awards	Part 2 para 3(2)(e)	
An explanation of why any entitlement of a director to share options or LTIP awards are not subject to performance conditions	Part 2 para 3(2)(f)	
Explanation of the relative importance of elements of each director's terms and conditions relating to remuneration which are and which are not related to performance	Part 2 para 3(3)	
Summary and explanation of policy on the duration of contracts with directors and notice periods and termination payments under such contracts	Part 2 para 3(4)	
Include in above all directors serving at any time from the end of the financial year to the date the Directors' Remuneration Report is laid before the company in general meeting	Part 2 para 3(5)	
4 Performance Graph		
A performance line graph joining up the points representing the total shareholder return ('TSR') on the class of equity share capital which caused them to fall within the definition of a 'quoted company' and the TSR of a hypothetical holding of shares of the same kinds and number as those by reference to which a broad equity market index is calculated (which should be stated and reasons given for selecting that index)	Part 2 para 4(1)	
The graph should be prepared to represent each relevant financial year in the relevant period (default five financial years, less if have been listed for a shorter period)	Part 2 para 4(2),(3)	

	Company X	
Source: Directors' Remuneration Report Regulations (Schedule 7A)	Reference	Checklist
TSR must be calculated using a fair method (and the same method for each holding) which takes as its starting point the percentage change in the market price of the holding over the relevant period and makes provision for any replacement of shares in the holding by shares of a different description	Part 2 para 4(4)(a)(c)	
The TSR calculation in the above assumes that any benefit (in particular dividends) of shares of the same kind as in the holding are added to the holding at the time the benefit becomes receivable	Part 2 para 4(4)(b)(i), (5)(a), (6)	
The TSR calculation in the above assumes that any benefit of cash and an amount equal to the benefit not in cash or in shares is applied at the time the benefit becomes receivable in the purchase at their market price of shares of the same kind as in the holding and the shares purchased are added to the holding at that time	Part 2 para 5(b)	
The TSR calculation in the above assumes that where the shareholder has a liability (as a result of a share award or option exercise) to a company (or another company of whose capital the shares in the holding form part), shares (in such numbers that the market price equals the liability) are sold from the holding immediately before the liability is due to be satisfied	Part 2 para 4(4)(b)(ii), (7),(8)	
5 Service Contracts		
Details of date of contracts, unexpired terms, notice periods, provisions to enable compensation payable on early termination to be estimated	Part 2 para 5(1)	
An explanation of significant awards made to any past directors	Part 2 para 5(2)	

	Company X	
	Reference	Checklist
Source: Directors' Remuneration Report Regulations (Schedule 7A)		
PART 3 – INFORMATION SUBJECT TO AUDIT		
6 Amount of each director's emoluments and compensation in the relevant financial year		
For each director of the company who was a director at any time during the Year, disclose each of the following in respect of qualifying services for the Year; (a) total salary, bonuses and fees paid or receivable; (b) total expense allowance payments that are chargeable to UK income tax paid or receivable e.g. housing allowance; (c) total amount paid or receivable in respect of any compensation for loss of office and other payments in connection with a termination; and (d) total estimated value and nature of any other non-cash benefits received as emoluments but excluding share options, LTIP entitlements, pension benefits and excess pension benefits, compensation for loss of office and payments to third parties each of which have to be disclosed separately (see below). (e) total of the sums in a) to c) above.	Part 3 para 6(1), (2)	
The directors' remuneration report shall also state the nature of the element of the remuneration which is not in cash	Part 3 para 6(1), (3)	
The information required in (1) and (2) should be presented in tabular format	Part 3 para 6(1), (4)	
7–9 Share options		
For each director of the Company at any time in the Year disclose; (a) the number of shares under option; (i) at the beginning of the Year or, if later, on the date of the appointment of the director of the Company, and	Part 3 paras 7–9	

Source: Directors' Remuneration Report Regulations (Schedule 7A)	Company X	
	Reference	Checklist
(ii) at the end of the Year or, if earlier, on the cessation of the director's appointment, in each case differentiating between share options having different terms and conditions;		
(b) information identifying options awarded, exercised, expired unexercised and whose terms and conditions have been varied in the Year;		
(c) for each share option that is unexpired at any time in the Year;		
(i) price paid, if any, for its award,		
(ii) exercise price,		
(iii) vesting date, and		
(iv) expiry date;		
(d) description of any variation to the terms and conditions of a share option made in the Year;		
(e) a summary of any performance criteria (including any variation made during the Year) which the award or exercise of a share option is conditional;		
(f) for each share option that has been exercised during the Year, the market price of the shares at the time of exercise;		
(g) for each share option that is unexpired at the end of the Year; the market price at the end of that Year, and the highest and lowest market prices during that Year.		
For the purposes of disclosure share options may be aggregated and (instead of disclosing prices/dates for each share option) disclosure may be made of weighted average prices/ranges of dates for aggregations of share options. Aggregation is not permitted of:	Part 3 para 9 (1), (2)	
(a) share options in respect of shares whose market price at the end of the financial year is below the option exercise price, with		
(b) share options in respect of shares whose market price at the end of the relevant financial year is equal to, or exceeds, the option exercise price.		

Source: Directors' Remuneration Report Regulations (Schedule 7A)	Company X	
	Reference	Checklist
The information required should be presented in tabular format		
10–11 Long-term incentive schemes		

For each director of the Company at any time in the Year disclose;
(a) details of the scheme interests at the beginning of the Year (or, if later, on the date of the appointment as a director) and at the end of the Year (or, if earlier, on the cessation of the director's appointment);
(b) the number of shares, market price of shares on award and performance conditions of scheme interests awarded during the Year;
(c) for each scheme interest;
  (i) the end of the performance period (or, if there is more than one period, the end of the last);
  (ii) a description of any variation to the terms and conditions of the scheme interests during the Year;
(d) for each scheme interest that has vested in the Year;
  (i) the number of shares, the date on which the scheme interest was awarded, the market price of each of the shares when the scheme interest was awarded and when it vested and details of performance conditions.
  (ii) the amount of any money, and the value of any other assets, that have become receivable in respect of the interest.
	Part 3 paras 10-11	

The information required should be presented in tabular format	Part 3 para 10(3)	

Source: Directors' Remuneration Report Regulations (Schedule 7A)	Company X	
	Reference	Checklist
Long-term incentive scheme' means an agreement or arrangement under which money or assets may become receivable by a person and which includes one or more qualifying conditions with respect to service or performance that cannot be fulfilled within a single financial year. Any bonus, compensation in respect of loss of office, payments for breach of contract and other termination payments and retirement benefits should be disregarded for this purpose.	Part 3 para 10(5)	
12 Pensions		
In relation to defined benefit disclose: (a) details of any changes during the relevant financial year in the directors accrued benefits under the scheme and details of the accrued benefits as at the end of that year (b) the transfer value as at the end of the financial year and at the end of the previous financial year (c) the increase in the transfer value over the year after deducting any members contribution	Part 3 para 12(1-2)	
For each person who has served as a director of the Company during the year, and who has become entitled to rights under a money purchase pension scheme in respect of qualifying services disclose details of any contribution to the scheme in respect of the person that is paid or payable by the Company for the Year or paid by the Company in the year for another financial year.	Part 3 para 12(3)	

	Company X	
	Reference	Checklist
Source: Directors' Remuneration Report Regulations (Schedule 7A)		
13 Excess retirement benefits of directors and past directors		
For each director of the Company at any time during, or before the beginning of the Year disclose the amount of retirement benefits (in respect of qualifying services) paid under pension schemes in excess of entitlements due when first payable or 31 March 1997, whichever is the latest	Part 3 para 13(1-2)	
Amounts paid or receivable under a pension scheme need not be included as 'retirement benefits' if (a) the funding of the scheme was such that the amounts were, or, as the case may be, could have been paid without recourse to additional contributions; and (b) amounts were paid to or receivable by all pensioner members of the scheme on the same basis	Part 3 para 13(3)	
Retirement benefits include non-cash benefits and the estimated money value of the benefit and its nature should be reported.	Part 3 para 13(4)	
14 Compensation for past directors		
Details of any significant award made in the Year to any person who had previously been a director of the Company including compensation for loss of office and pensions but excluding any sums which have already been reported.	Part 3 para 14	
15 Sums paid to third parties in respect of a director's services		
For each director of the Company at any time during the Year, the nature and aggregate amount of any consideration paid to or receivable by third parties (i.e. the person himself or a person connected with him or a body corporate controlled by him, and the company or any such other undertaking) for making available the qualifying services of the director or in connection with the management of the affairs of the Company or any such undertaking.	Part 3 para 15	

Appendix 3
NAPF Corporate Governance Policy and Checklist

The NAPF Corporate Governance Policy, updated in January 2005, expands upon the Combined Code and, in some instances, gives specific voting guidance. The checklist provided enables the Remuneration Committee to check compliance with the provisions and anticipate the likely voting recommendations of the NAPF on issues that breach the guidelines. The Code Provisions that are most directly relevant to the Remuneration Committee are indicated by [•] symbols, as are those that relate to shareholder relations.

Source: NAPF Corporate Governance Policy – where this expands the Combined Code or has specific voting guidance	Reference	Company X			
		Board	Appointments and Nomination Committee	Remuneration Policy and Remuneration Committee	Shareholder Relations
The board should include NEDs of sufficient calibre and number for views to carry significant weight	A1	•			
The board has responsibility for planned and progressive refreshing of the board and committees. This should be reviewed annually, with formal evaluation of skills, knowledge and experience on board.	A2	•			
It is good practice if, for re-elections, board confirms to shareholders that (a) board development plans are reviewed annually, (b) they involve an objecive and comprehensive evaluation of the balance of skills, knowledge and experience, and (c) the proposed re-election is consistent with results of this review	A2	•			
A detailed explanation is required if a board does not report compliance with the requirement for at least half the board (or 2 directors, for smaller companies) to be independent NEDs for ALL the first year under the new Code	A3	•			
Further explanation is required on 'independence' in terms of cross directorships and significant links	A4	•			

Source: NAPF Corporate Governance Policy – where this expands the Combined Code or has specific voting guidance	Reference	Board	Company X		
			Appointments and Nomination Committee	Remuneration Policy and Remuneration Committee	Shareholder Relations
Board must identify in the annual report those directors viewed as independent	A5	•			
An executive director should not be a NED of more than one other Listed Company (Code says FTSE100). Policy on multiple appointments of executives and non-executives directors should be defined. If director holds excess appointments, on re-election, board should explain policy and application	A6	•			
Where director changes role (to chairman; or from executive to non-executive; or non-executive to executive) good practice is to propose the director for re-election. From 2005 AGM onwards, failure could lead to a recommendation against the re-election of a Director who was not proposed for re-election at the first AGM following the change in role. Alternatively, the NAPF may recommend that either the Chairman of the Nominations Committee or the Chairman of the Board should not be re-elected at the AGM at which the opportunity to propose the re-election of the Director changing their role could have been taken by the Board, but was not.	A7	•			

Source: NAPF Corporate Governance Policy – where this expands the Combined Code or has specific voting guidance	Reference	Board	Company X		
			Appointments and Nomination Committee	Remuneration Policy and Remuneration Committee	Shareholder Relations
It is good practice that a Director should not be on a committee for more than 6 yrs and committee membership should reflect skills and maximise diversity. Smaller companies might want to consider planned rotation	A8	•			
Directors should be absent from discussions on their successors to the board or board roles	A9	•			
If board size permits, SID should not chair remuneration committee or audit committee and different independent NEDs should chair the 3 main committees (or in smaller companies, the 2 independent NEDs should chair remuneration committee and audit and the company chairman nomination)	A9	•			
NAPF may recommend a vote against re-election where insufficient details are provided (around board rationale, performance evaluation, commitment and effectiveness)	A10	•			
NAPF may recommend a vote against re-election where terms of appointment are not available for inspection	A11	•			

Source: NAPF Corporate Governance Policy – where this expands the Combined Code or has specific voting guidance	Reference	Company X			
		Board	Appointments and Nomination Committee	Remuneration Policy and Remuneration Committee	Shareholder Relations
If at the 2005 AGM nomination committee chairman is neither company chairman nor independent NED could lead to a recommendation to vote against	B1		•		
If the majority of the nomination committee are not independent NEDs this would normally lead to recommendation to vote against	B2		•		
If terms of reference are not available or not up to date this could lead to a recommendation to vote against	B3 and B4		•		
The annual report should give details on (a) structure committee start/end year, (b) reason for change, (c) summary of terms of reference, (d) number of meetings, (e) secretary, (f) major matters dealt with, and (g) for any appointments, process including search and advertising	B5		•		
At AGM, committee chairman should explain structure and membership. Substance of questions/answers should be put on website within 2 days and made available on request to Shareholders	B6		•		•

Source: NAPF Corporate Governance Policy – where this expands the Combined Code or has specific voting guidance	Reference	Company X			
		Board	Appointments and Nomination Committee	Remuneration Policy and Remuneration Committee	Shareholder Relations
Good practice is to confirm in annual report that the existing chairman is are not involved in the selection of a successor. Failure may lead to recommendation to vote against	C1	•			
If chairman is not independent on appointment this may lead to recommendation to vote against	C2	•			
Company chairman should not be chairman of more than one large and complex company (Combined Code says FTSE100 company). May lead to recommendation to vote against	C3	•			
If a chairman is also CEO, will normally recommend a vote against	C4	•			
Where a CEO becomes chairman this will normally recommend a vote against if not satisfied by rationale, consultation and search process. New chairman should be proposed at next AGM	C6	•			
Senior Independent Director and responsibilities should be identified in annual report	C7	•			

Source: NAPF Corporate Governance Policy – where this expands the Combined Code or has specific voting guidance	Reference	Board	Company X Appointments and Nomination Committee	Remuneration Policy and Remuneration Committee	Shareholder Relations
Use of alternate or corporate directors inappropriate	D1, D2	•			
Monthly/annual time commitment of NED should be agreed by chairman and nomination committee. Failure to consistently meet time requirements should be addressed by them	D3	•	•		
Chairman or SID should make preparations for, and attend any meetings required between major shareholders and new NEDs	D4	•			•
Where a NED resigns due to company's performance, policies or governance, reasons should be agreed, set out in regulatory announcement and made available on the website	D5	•			
The company secretary should be an employee and should not be an executive director. If roles are not separate this should be explained in annual report	E1, E2	•			
On change of secretary, policy for appointment and removal should be confirmed in the annual report and there should be immediate announcement on regulatory service and then company website with rationale for resignation/removal	E3, E4, E5	•			

| Source: NAPF Corporate Governance Policy – where this expands the Combined Code or has specific voting guidance | Reference | Company X | | | |
		Board	Appointments and Nomination Committee	Remuneration Policy and Remuneration Committee	Shareholder Relations
Where a director is unable to attend number of board meetings, NAPF recommends explanation in the annual report to avoid uncertainty over commitment	F1	•			
Good practice to announce full voting results immediately after AGM on regulatory service and website	G1				•
If remuneration committee size and composition does not meet the Code recommendations by 2005 i.e. because the Executive Director is a member of the Committee this will normally lead to a voting recommendation against the approval of the Remuneration Report. If a Non-Executive Director who is not considered independent is a member of the committee then a voting recommendation against the re-election of the Director and/or a vote against the approval of the Remuneration Report	H1-3			•	
If terms of reference are not available or updated this could lead to recommendation to vote against	H4			•	
In terms of engagement of appointed remuneration consultants should be available on website and on request, with details of other work done for the company	H5		•		

Source: NAPF Corporate Governance Policy – where this expands the Combined Code or has specific voting guidance	Reference	Company X			
		Board	Appointments and Nomination Committee	Remuneration Policy and Remuneration Committee	Shareholder Relations
If consultants provide other services, it should be minimalised, disclosed and explained to remuneration committee	H5			•	
Members should understand incentive schemes, committee's remuneration policy, its application, cost to the company and potential value to participant. Chairman should be available to discuss these with shareholders and at AGM	H6			•	•
If there is not a Remuneration Committee then there will normally be a vote against the approval of the Remuneration Report	H7			•	
The Board and remuneration committee should take account of voting results on the annual report and the views of shareholders	I1	•		•	
At the AGM, committee chairman should explain structure and membership. Substance of questions/answers should be put on website within 2 days and made available on request to Shareholders	J1			•	•

Source: NAPF Corporate Governance Policy – where this expands the Combined Code or has specific voting guidance	Reference	Company X			
		Board	Appointments and Nomination Committee	Remuneration Policy and Remuneration Committee	Shareholder Relations
Company should disclose the average total annual remuneration of directors and of non board employees in the financial year; the policy with respect to the ratio between these; actual ratio and comparable figures for the previous year or demonstrate how the Remuneration Committee has dealt with this matter	K2			•	
Remuneration committee should be aware of the relationship between employment benefits offered to executive directors and other senior executives and those available more widely with respect to performance incentives, pensions and other employment benefits	K2			•	
Good practice to limit increase of non performance pay to the company average (excluding executive directors) and strongly link performance related elements to above average and upper quartile performance	K2			•	
Use of an external comparator group comprising less than 10 companies to benchmark current remuneration levels are set and apply future remuneration policy is unlikely to be satisfactory	K3			•	

Source: NAPF Corporate Governance Policy – where this expands the Combined Code or has specific voting guidance	Reference	Board	Company X		
			Appointments and Nomination Committee	Remuneration Policy and Remuneration Committee	Shareholder Relations
The methodology used to select the comparator group should be disclosed in remuneration report, as well as the list of companies in the group	K3			•	
Good practice to limit 'spiral' ratcheting by abiding by the principles of 'above median remuneration' only for 'above median performance' and where rankings against comparators are used, an adjustment is made to take account of the extent to which the company has exceeded the performance of the company immediately below it	K4			•	
Ahead of an executive appointment, remuneration committee should consider director's contractual protection in light of level of remuneration to be received	K5			•	
If a director has no contract or contract with length/notice period of more than one year could lead to recommendation to vote against	K5 and 6		•		

Source: NAPF Corporate Governance Policy – where this expands the Combined Code or has specific voting guidance	Reference	Company X			
		Board	Appointments and Nomination Committee	Remuneration Policy and Remuneration Committee	Shareholder Relations
Remuneration committee should have a clear policy on directors' contract and termination arrangements and be able to quantify the cost of termination at any time in future. Compensation should only relate to base salary. It is the Board and Remuneration Committee's responsibility to decide best route to minimise costs (e.g. liquidated, phased)	K7	•		•	
On Change in Control, no remuneration element should allow for abnormally high or max pay out - only incentive due at time should be awarded. Any enhancements should be disclosed and may lead to recommendation to vote against	K8			•	
Remuneration report should state if executive director departure is voluntary or a termination. Any termination payments (including non-compete) or additional rights (e.g. pension) should be disclosed and justified	K9 and K10			•	
Ex-gratia and other non-contractual payments are not normally appropriate. Size and rationale for any such payments should be given in the remuneration report. May lead to vote against recommendation	K11			•	

Source: NAPF Corporate Governance Policy – where this expands the Combined Code or has specific voting guidance	Reference	Company X			
		Board	Appointments and Nomination Committee	Remuneration Policy and Remuneration Committee	Shareholder Relations
Remuneration committee should consider pension consequences of changes to pensionable pay and take pension costs into account when assessing total remuneration	K12			•	
It is good practice to publish in the annual report clear explanations of all relevant pensions matters and policy with regard to a new regime	K12			•	
Remuneration committee should confirm in the annual report that it has appropriate policies and procedures in place to monitor the size of potential awards	K13			•	
Remuneration Committees should remunerate the Chairman and Non-Executive Directors appropriately	K14			•	
Pay for Non-Executive Directors' fees may include shares, or pay partly in shares. However, the award of share options or any other geared incentives to Non-Executive Directors is not considered good practice	K14			•	

Source: NAPF Corporate Governance Policy – where this expands the Combined Code or has specific voting guidance	Reference	Company X			
		Board	Appointments and Nomination Committee	Remuneration Policy and Remuneration Committee	Shareholder Relations
Requirement for Directors to own shares. For Non-Executives, judgement should be used to ensure that the required shareholding does not compromise independence	K15			•	
Base salaries of executive directors at the financial year end (i.e. current base pay) should be disclosed and if there are significant differences in these compared to the date of the annual report, these should be disclosed	L1			•	
The remuneration committee should carefully consider consequence of salary increases on variable incentives and pension, and strongly resist increases above company average	L1			•	
Remuneration report should include bonus amount paid to each executive director plus description of performance targets achieved, explanation of link between performance and bonus paid, and max level of bonus. Any change in targets over the year should also be explained	L2			•	

Source: NAPF Corporate Governance Policy – where this expands the Combined Code or has specific voting guidance	Reference	Company X Board	Appointments and Nomination Committee	Remuneration Policy and Remuneration Committee	Shareholder Relations
Annual bonus payments should be directly linked to stretching performance targets at the start of the period to which they relate and a clear explanation should be given to shareholders of the manner in which these performance targets are tied in with the compay's shorter-term objectives	L2			•	
NAPF does not support transaction bonuses linked to acquisition as this should be rewarded through existing LTIs. A special bonus on disposal may, exceptionally, be appropriate	L3			•	
Long-term incentive schemes should closely align the rewards available to executive directors and shareholders and a clear statement to shareholders on how performance targets are tied to the company's longer-term strategic objectives should be given	L4			•	
NAPF believes LTI schemes should be uncomplicated, with upside rewards and downside risks aligned to shareholders, and supports schemes that encourage retention of shares after vesting	L4			•	

Source: NAPF Corporate Governance Policy – where this expands the Combined Code or has specific voting guidance	Reference	Company X			
		Board	Appointments and Nomination Committee	Remuneration Policy and Remuneration Committee	Shareholder Relations
Matching shares' should be subject to additional performance conditions over at least 3 yrs	L4			•	
Executives should retain a meaningful investment in the company by avoiding, exchanging, at the Company's expense their vesting shares in the company for a diversified portfolio of shares	L4			•	
The basis of calculation of the economic value of the long-term incentive (rather than value) should be explained	L4			•	
The relationship between performance targets and rewards/ awards made in the financial year and potentially available to directors in future years should be explained.	L5			•	
Total cost and potential value of awards made during the year and outstanding awards should be disclosed in the remuneration report	L5			•	
Directors should preferably participate in only one share scheme at a time. Where they participate in more than one scheme, this must be a part of a well considered remuneration policy and the remuneration committee should pay specific attention to combined scale of potential awards	L6			•	

Source: NAPF Corporate Governance Policy – where this expands the Combined Code or has specific voting guidance	Reference	Board	Appointments and Nomination Committee	Remuneration Policy and Remuneration Committee	Shareholder Relations
				Company X	
A clear explanation should be given to shareholders explaining how performance targets are tied with the company's longer-term strategic objectives	L7			•	
For STI the minimum performance threshold should not be below the average/median performance achieved in the preceding 3 yrs	L7			•	
For LTI based on performance relative to other companies, the minimum performance threshold should not be below the average/median of the benchmark group	L7			•	
Rewards close to minimum performance level should be modest and the greater the potential reward the more stretching the condition should be	L7			•	
Max awards under each incentive scheme (including annual bonus and LTI) should be stated in the annual report with respect to payments and awards made in the financial year and in place at the end of the financial year	L7			•	

Source: NAPF Corporate Governance Policy – where this expands the Combined Code or has specific voting guidance	Reference	Company X			
		Board	Appointments and Nomination Committee	Remuneration Policy and Remuneration Committee	Shareholder Relations
NAPF prefers the use of sliding scale to a single hurdle	L7			•	
Performance period for LTI should be a min of 3 yrs (5 yrs being the NAPF preferred length)	L8			•	
Changes to the performance conditions of all LTIs should be subject to shareholder approval	L9			•	
New schemes should not include any provision for retesting. Retesting in existing schemes may be allowed if start date does not change, the condition becomes more demanding and there is full disclosure. In 2006, a vote against the Remuneration Report will be recommended	L10			•	
Share incentive awards should be phased	L11			•	
It is not good practice to fund political parties or organisations and would normally lead to a voting recommendation against resolutions	M11			•	

Source: NAPF Corporate Governance Policy – where this expands the Combined Code or has specific voting guidance	Reference	Company X			
		Board	Appointments and Nomination Committee	Remuneration Policy and Remuneration Committee	Shareholder Relations
Changes to the company's Memorandum and Articles is supported provided that it is clearly demonstrated by the Board that any changes will not detract from shareholder value or materially reduce shareholder rights and that non-routine changes are not 'bundled' into a single resolution when they cover seperate issues	N1			•	
Shareholder approval must be sought for at least one dividend payment, if more than one, and preferably the last, or 'Final' dividend. Exceptions may be made if there is evidence that changing to voting practices would significantly delay dividends payments or would be a material disadvantage to shareholde	O1			•	
The remuneration committee should ensure policies are in place to monitor dilution levels (total 10% over 10 yrs and, for discretionary schemes, 5% over 10 yrs). Lapsed and exercised options cannot be excluded. The NAPF will recommend a vote against any attempt to increase this limit beyond 5%	P3			•	

Source: NAPF Corporate Governance Policy – where this expands the Combined Code or has specific voting guidance	Reference	Company X			
		Board	Appointments and Nomination Committee	Remuneration Policy and Remuneration Committee	Shareholder Relations
NAPF considers the use of Treasury shares to be no different from the use of newly issued shares. NAPF will not recommend a vote for resolution on the market purchase of shares unless company confirms whether shares are being cancelled or held as Treasury shares which are subject to dilution limits on re-use for share based schemes	P4			•	
It is good practice for companies to disclose for discretionary and non-discretionary schemes, number of shares committed (a) at start of year, (b) during year, (c) end of year, (d) proportion of options end of year compared to 5% and 10% ceilings	P5			•	
The NAPFs policy will usually lead to a voting recommendation against a resolution permitting market purchases of the company's own shares, unless the company confirms (1) whether the shares are being repurchased are to be cancelled or held as Treasury Shares and (2) if the latter will be made within the overall 10% anti-dilution limit for such share issues	P6			•	

Appendix 4
ABI and NAPF Contracts Best Practice and Checklist

In a joint statement updated in December 2004, the ABI and NAPF set out their expectations that boards should give careful consideration to the risk that negotiation of inappropriate executive contracts can lead to situations where failure is rewarded. The checklist will enable the Remuneration Committee to identify areas of non-compliance and while no specific voting guidance was given with regard to these provisions it is a fair assumption that any breaches might form the basis of subsequent dialogue with the ABI, NAPF and various institutional investors.

Source: ABI and NAPF Contracts Best Practice	Reference	Company X			
		Board	Appointments and Nomination Committee	Remuneration Policy and Remuneration Committee	Shareholder Relations
Contract design should not commit companies to payment for failure	2.1			•	
Companies should have a clear, considered policy on directors' contracts which should be clearly stated in the remuneration report	2.2			•	
Executives objectives should be clear as to make it easier to determine underperformance. Where possible, objectives should be made public	2.3			•	
Investors do not expect executives to be automatically entitled to bonuses: from the outset boards should therefore establish a clear link between performance and bonus and other elements of variable pay	2.4			•	•
In exceptional circumstances, a longer notice period than 1 year may be appropriate e.g. new CEO to troubled company. Should be justified to shareholders and revert to best practice at first opportunity	2.6			•	
Courts have taken account of variable pay when making awards to departing executives. This can be limited through clear attachment of performance conditions specifying that part of the bonus for retention purposes	2.7			•	

Source: ABI and NAPF Contracts Best Practice	Reference	Board	Company X		
			Appointments and Nomination Committee	Remuneration Policy and Remuneration Committee	Shareholder Relations
Boards should consider relative merits of different approaches (e.g. phased payments, liquidated damages and reliance on mitigation), follow chosen approach and justify it to shareholders	3.1	•		•	•
Phased payments are a welcome innovation. Allowing the contract to run off may also obviate need for pension enhancements	3.2			•	
Shareholders do not believe liquidated damages approach is generally desirable. Boards which adopt it should justify their decision and consider modifying it e.g. agree to go to arbitration to decide how much should be paid	3.3	•		•	•
Where mitigation is sole approach, shareholders expect reassurance that board has taken steps to ensure that full benefit is gained	3.4	•		•	•
Boards should be aware of statutory discipline procedure under Employment Act 2002 and be prepared to use disciplinary procedures, if deemed necessary	3.5	•			

Source: ABI and NAPF Contracts Best Practice	Reference	Board	Company X		
			Appointments and Nomination Committee	Remuneration Policy and Remuneration Committee	Shareholder Relations
Contracts should make clear that in wake of disciplinary procedure a shorter notice period would apply	3.6	•			
Companies should consider a safeguard for extreme cases e.g. no compensation for financial failure	3.7	•		•	
Except in highly exceptional circumstances, there should be no additional protection for Change in Control that would exceed 1 yr max under the Combined Code	3.8			•	
Companies should consider other options e.g. compensation paid by reference to shares, with amount of shares set at start of employment. Compensation paid in reference to shares should be made in cash rather than shares	3.9			•	
Use of shareholding targets is likely to be effective in aligning financial interest of executives with those of shareholders	3.10			•	•
Board should state full economic cost of pension enhancement at earliest opportunity. Boards should not support pension payments without being fully aware of costs	4.1	•		•	

Source: ABI and NAPF Contracts Best Practice	Reference	Board	Company X Appointments and Nomination Committee	Company X Remuneration Policy and Remuneration Committee	Company X Shareholder Relations
In case of enhanced pensions, Boards must disclose the cost of pensions, justify choice and demonstrate chosen alternative has least overall cost	4.2	•		•	
Contracts should state that pensions will not be enhanced in the event of early retirement unless the board is satisfied that executive's objective met or enhancement merited. Shareholders may vote against if not satisfied	4.3			•	•
Boards should have clear and explicit contracts policy, including how to calculate the cost of severance at start and ensure all payment take account of executives performance against objectives	5.1	•		•	
Contracts should be readily available for shareholders to inspect, together with side letters relating to pension and severance terms	5.2			•	•

Appendix 5
ICSA Remuneration Committee Terms of Reference

In response to the Combined Code recommendations, the ICSA has proposed model terms of reference for Remuneration Committees. These were drawn up by reference to senior company secretaries and reflect best practice as carried out in some of the country's leading companies.

The Combined Code on Corporate Governance (the Combined Code) states that:

'There should be a formal and transparent procedure for developing policy on executive remuneration and for fixing the remuneration packages of individual directors.'

It goes on to state that:

'The board should establish a Remuneration Committee ...[which] should make available its terms of reference, explaining its role and the authority delegated to it by the board.'

As with many aspects of corporate governance, the above principles make it clear that, not only should companies go through a formal process of considering executive remuneration, but they must be seen to be doing so in a fair and thorough manner. It is, therefore, essential that the Remuneration Committee is properly constituted with a clear remit and identified authority.

The Combined Code recommends the Committee be made up of at least three independent non-executive directors (although two is permissible for smaller companies).

Although not a provision in the Combined Code, the Higgs review states as good practice in its Non-Code Recommendations, that the company secretary (or their designee) should act as secretary to the Committee.

It is the company secretary's responsibility to ensure that the board and its committees are properly constituted and advised. There also needs to be a clear co-ordination between the main board and the various committees where the company secretary would normally act as a valued intermediary.

The frequency with which the Remuneration Committee needs to meet will vary from company to company and may change from time to time. It is, however, clear that it must meet close to the year end; to review the Remuneration Report which is required to be prepared under the Directors' Remuneration Report Regulations

2002 and be submitted to shareholders with or as part of the company's annual report for their approval at the AGM.

We would recommend that the Committee should meet at least twice a year in order to discharge its responsibilities properly.

The list of duties we have proposed are those contained within the Summary of Principle Duties of the Remuneration Committee which ICSA helped compile for the Higgs review and which are now appended to the Combined Code. Some companies may wish to add to this list and some smaller companies may need to modify it in other ways. The Combined Code also states that the Chairman of the Committee should attend the AGM prepared to respond to any questions that may be raised by shareholders on matters within the Committee's area of responsibility.

There is clearly a need for a guiding document for the effective operation of the Remuneration Committee. This has led the ICSA to produce this Guidance Note proposing model terms of reference for a Remuneration Committee. The document draws on the experience of senior Company Secretaries and best practice as carried out in some of the country's leading companies.

The Combined Code also requires that the terms of reference of the Remuneration Committee, explaining its role and the authority delegated to it by the board, be made available on request and placed on the company's website.

References to 'the Committee' shall mean the Remuneration Committee. References to 'the board'shall mean the board of directors. The square brackets contain recommendations which are in line with best practice but which may need to be changed to suit the circumstances of the particular organisation.

1. Membership

1.1   Members of the Committee shall be appointed by the board, on the recommendation of the Nomination Committee in consultation with the Chairman of the Remuneration Committee. The Committee shall be made up of at least [3] members, all of whom are independent non-executive directors.

1.2   Only members of the Committee have the right to attend Committee meetings. However, other individuals such as the Chief Executive, the head of human resources and external advisers may be invited to attend for all or part of any meeting as and when appropriate.

1.3   Appointments to the Committee shall be for a period of up to three years, which may be extended for two further three-year periods, provided the director remains independent.

1.4 The board shall appoint the Committee Chairman who shall be an independent non-executive director. In the absence of the Committee Chairman and/or an appointed deputy, the remaining members present shall elect one of themselves to chair the meeting. The Chairman of the board shall not be Chairman the Committee.

2. Secretary

2.1 The company secretary or their nominee shall act as the secretary of the Committee.

3. Quorum

3.1 The quorum necessary for the transaction of business shall be [2]. A duly convened meeting of the Committee at which a quorum is present shall be competent to exercise all or any of the authorities, powers and discretions vested in or exercisable by the Committee.

4. Meetings

4.1 The Committee shall meet [at least twice a year][quarterly on the first Wednesday in each of January, April, July and October] and at such other times as the Chairman of the Committee shall require.

5. Notice of Meetings

5.1 Meetings of the Committee shall be summoned by the secretary of the Committee at the request of any of its members.

5.2 Unless otherwise agreed, notice of each meeting confirming the venue, time and date together with an agenda of items to be discussed, shall be forwarded to each member of the Committee, any other person required to attend and all other non-executive directors, no later than [5] working days before the date of the meeting. Supporting papers shall be sent to Committee members and to other attendees as appropriate, at the same time.

6. Minute of Meetings

6.1 The secretary shall minute the proceedings and resolutions of all Committee meetings, including the names of those present and in attendance.

6.2 Minutes of Committee meetings shall be circulated promptly to all members of the Committee and, once agreed, to all members of the board, unless a conflict of interest exists.

7. Annual General Meeting

7.1 The Chairman of the Committee shall attend the Annual General Meeting prepared to respond to any shareholder questions on the Committee's activities.

8. Duties

The Committee shall:

8.1 determine and agree with the board the framework or broad policy for the remuneration of the company's Chief Executive, Chairman, the executive directors, the company secretary and such other members of the executive management as it is designated to consider. The remuneration of non-executive directors shall be a matter for the Chairman and the executive members of the board. No director or manager shall be involved in any decisions as to their own remuneration;

8.2 in determining such policy, take into account all factors which it deems necessary. The objective of such policy shall be to ensure that members of the executive management of the company are provided with appropriate incentives to encourage enhanced performance and are, in a fair and responsible manner, rewarded for their individual contributions to the success of the company;

8.3 review the ongoing appropriateness and relevance of the remuneration policy;

8.4 approve the design of, and determine targets for, any performance related pay schemes operated by the company and approve the total annual payments made under such schemes;

8.5 review the design of all share incentive plans for approval by the board and shareholders. For any such plans, determine each year whether awards will be made, and if so, the overall amount of such awards, the individual awards to executive directors and other senior executives and the performance targets to be used;

8.6 determine the policy for, and scope of, pension arrangements for each executive director and other senior executives;

8.7 ensure that contractual terms on termination, and any payments made, are fair to the individual, and the company, that failure is not rewarded and that the duty to mitigate loss is fully recognised;

8.8 within the terms of the agreed policy and in consultation with the Chairman and/or Chief Executive as appropriate, determine the total individual remuneration package of each executive director and other senior executives including bonuses, incentive payments and share options or other share awards;

8.9 in determining such packages and arrangements, give due regard to any relevant legal requirements, the provisions and recommendations in the Combined Code and the UK Listing Authority's Listing Rules and associated guidance;

8.10 review and note annually the remuneration trends across the company or group;

8.11 oversee any major changes in employee benefits structures throughout the company or group;

8.12 agree the policy for authorising claims for expenses from the Chief Executive and Chairman;

8.13 ensure that all provisions regarding disclosure of remuneration including pensions, as set out in the Directors 'Remuneration Report Regulations 2002 and the Combined Code are fulfilled; and

8.14 be exclusively responsible for establishing the selection criteria, selecting, appointing and setting the terms of reference for any remuneration consultants who advise the committee: and to obtain reliable, up-to-date information about remuneration in other companies. The Committee shall have full authority to commission any reports or surveys which it deems necessary to help it fulfil its obligations.

9. Reporting Responsibilities

9.1 The Committee Chairman shall report formally to the board on its proceedings after each meeting on all matters within its duties and responsibilities.

9.2 The Committee shall make whatever recommendations to the board it deems appropriate on any area within its remit where action or improvement is needed.

9.3   The Committee shall produce an annual report of the company's remuneration policy and practices which will form part of the company's annual report and ensure each year that it is put to shareholders for approval at the AGM.

10. Other

10.1 The Committee shall, at least once a year, review its own performance, constitution and terms of reference to ensure it is operating at maximum effectiveness and recommend any changes it considers necessary to the board for approval.

11. Authority

11.1 The Committee is authorised by the board to seek any information it requires from any employee of the company in order to perform its duties.

11.2 In connection with its duties the Committee is authorised by the board to obtain, at the company's expense, any outside legal or other professional advice.

Appendix 6
Example of Remuneration Committee Meeting Agenda

A comprehensive agenda helps members stay focused on their job. However, the nature of Remuneration Committee responsibilities and the ever-changing environment in which companies operate make it difficult to determine a set agenda for each meeting. The committee should assess what is currently important, and develop its agenda accordingly.

Remuneration Committee meeting agenda

	Scheduled meetings			
	April/ May	July/ August	October/ November	January/ February
Constitution				
Review Remuneration Committee's terms of reference	■			
Review code of conduct		■		
Assess independence, knowledge and experience of members			■	
Establish number of meetings for the forthcoming year		■		
Remuneration Committee chair to establish meeting agenda and attendees required	■	■	■	■
Enhance remuneration knowledge – update on current remuneration issues	■	■	■	■
Assessment of remuneration information				
Review draft directors' remuneration report			■	
Review final results for the year				■

	Scheduled meetings			
	April/ May	July/ August	October/ November	January/ February
Review and recommend approval of directors' remuneration report				■
Review shareholder reactions to circular/annual report		■		
Market practice review		■		
Explore market trends and need for possible amendments to current arrangements (strategic review)		■		
Assessment of remuneration policy				
Review the ongoing appropriateness and relevance of the remuneration policy	■	■	■	■
Review of compliance with corporate governance regulations and codes	■	■	■	■
Consider results of remuneration strategy review				■
Perform initial pay review		■		
Finalise pay review			■	
Review of earnings under the annual bonus plan			■	
Finalise the targets for the annual bonus plan				■
Review of participation in the long-term incentive arrangements		■		
Review quanta to be awarded under long-term incentive arrangements	■			
Review of awards under the long-term incentive arrangements	■			
Review of awards vesting in relation to performance conditions	■		■	
Agree payout under short-term incentive arrangements				■

	Scheduled meetings			
	April/ May	July/ August	October/ November	January/ February
Agree awards under the long-term incentive arrangements	▓			
Finalise any plans to be put to shareholder vote				▓
Remuneration consultants				
Review terms of reference of any remuneration consultants and their other connections with the company	▓	▓	▓	▓
Other responsibilities	▓	▓	▓	▓
Consider business risks and internal controls relating to remuneration	▓	▓	▓	▓
Review report to shareholders on role and responsibilities of committee				▓
Perform self-assessment of remuneration committee performance			▓	
Review chief executive and chairman expenses	▓			
Maintain minutes and report to board	▓	▓	▓	▓

Appendix 7
Example of Remuneration Committee Self-assessment

Assessment of the Remuneration Committee

The self-assessment has been prepared on the basis that each Remuneration Committee member will complete it independently. The Remuneration Committee chairman would then lead discussion on the results of the questionnaire, focusing on those areas which clearly need improvement or where there is great variation in answers. Alternatively, the self-assessment could be undertaken as a facilitated group activity led by the Remuneration Committee chairman or an external party.

Remuneration committee chairmen may wish to give more weight to some aspects of the self-assessment than others. Appropriate weighting will be influenced by a number of factors including, but not limited to:

- the Committee's charter;

- the outcomes of previous self-assessments;

- the stage of maturity of the Remuneration Committee; and

- current and emerging business and economic factors.

The results of the self-assessment and any action plans arising should be reported to the board after discussion with the chairman of the board. The board should also make its own assessment of the performance of the Remuneration Committee's effectiveness on an annual basis.

| | | Rating | | | | | |
| | | Excellent | | | Poor | | |
	Yes/No/N/A	1	2	3	4	5	Comment
Terms of reference							
Have the Remuneration Committee's terms of reference been approved by the board?		☐	☐	☐	☐	☐	
Does the Remuneration Committee annually review its terms of reference and recommend any necessary changes to the board		☐	☐	☐	☐	☐	

			Rating				
			Excellent			Poor	
	Yes/No/N/A	1	2	3	4	5	Comment

Do the terms of reference include:

- determination of a policy for the remuneration of the executive directors and the chairman; ☐ ☐ ☐ ☐ ☐

- establishing performance-related pay scheme targets; ☐ ☐ ☐ ☐ ☐

- establishing the policy and scope of pension arrangements for each executive director; ☐ ☐ ☐ ☐ ☐

- reviewing the company's termination policy; ☐ ☐ ☐ ☐ ☐

- determination of total remuneration packages for individual executive directors; ☐ ☐ ☐ ☐ ☐

- provision of advice to the company on major changes in employee benefit structures; ☐ ☐ ☐ ☐ ☐

- agreeing the policy for authorising claims for expenses from the chief executive, chairman and other executive directors; ☐ ☐ ☐ ☐ ☐

- reviewing the appropriateness and relevance of the remuneration policy on a regular basis ☐ ☐ ☐ ☐ ☐

Membership and appointments

Does the Remuneration Committee consist independent non-executive directors ☐ ☐ ☐ ☐ ☐

Is the board chairman excluded from Remuneration Committee membership ☐ ☐ ☐ ☐ ☐

	Yes/No/N/A	Rating Excellent 1	2	3	Poor 4	5	Comment
Are Remuneration Committee members appointed by the board on the recommendation of the nomination committee (where there is one) in consultation with the Remuneration Committee chairman		☐	☐	☐	☐	☐	
Is Remuneration Committee membership restricted to a term no longer than three years (extendable by no more than two additional three-year periods)		☐	☐	☐	☐	☐	

Meetings

	Yes/No/N/A	1	2	3	4	5	Comment
Does the audit committee meet regularly (at least twice a year)		☐	☐	☐	☐	☐	
Are Remuneration Committee meetings well attended?							
Do Remuneration Committee meetings allow sufficient time for discussion and questions		☐	☐	☐	☐	☐	
Are meeting agendas and related background information circulated in a timely manner to enable full and proper consideration to be given to the issues?							
Is sufficient time allowed between Remuneration Committee meetings and board meetings to allow any work arising to be carried out and reported to the board as appropriate		☐	☐	☐	☐	☐	

	Rating					
	Excellent			Poor		
Yes/No/N/A	1	2	3	4	5	Comment

Training and resources

Does the Remuneration Committee have sufficient skills, experience, time and resources to undertake its duties	☐	☐	☐	☐	☐	
Is an induction programme (covering the role of the Remuneration Committee, its terms of reference and expected time commitment by members; an overview of the company's business; and the main business and financial dynamics and risks) provided for new Remuneration Committee members	☐	☐	☐	☐	☐	
Do Remuneration Committee members receive relevant training in current remuneration issues and related company law on an ongoing and timely basis	☐	☐	☐	☐	☐	
Do Remuneration Committee members have the opportunity to attend formal courses and conferences, internal company talks and seminars, and briefings by external advisers such as the company's auditors and lawyers	☐	☐	☐	☐	☐	
Does the Remuneration Committee have access to the services of the company secretary and staff	☐	☐	☐	☐	☐	
Are funds available to enable the Remuneration Committee to take independent legal, accounting or other advice when it reasonably believes it necessary to do so?	☐	☐	☐	☐	☐	

	Yes/No/N/A	Rating Excellent 1	2	3	Poor 4	5	Comment

Financial reporting

	Yes/No/N/A	1	2	3	4	5	Comment
Does the Remuneration Committee ensure that provisions regarding disclosure of remuneration, including pensions, set out in the Directors' Remuneration Report Regulations 2002, the UK Listing Authority's Listing Rules and the Combined Code are fulfilled		☐	☐	☐	☐	☐	

Relationship with the board

	Yes/No/N/A	1	2	3	4	5	Comment
Does the committee report to the full board after each meeting		☐	☐	☐	☐	☐	
Where there is disagreement between the remuneration committee and the board, is adequate time set aside for discussion of the issue with a view to resolving the disagreement		☐	☐	☐	☐	☐	
Where disagreements between the remuneration committee and the board cannot be resolved, does the remuneration committee have the right to report the issue to shareholders		☐	☐	☐	☐	☐	

Communications with shareholders

	Yes/No/N/A	1	2	3	4	5	Comment
Does the Remuneration Committee ensure that a report on its role and responsibilities, and the actions taken to discharge those responsibilities is included in the annual report and accounts?		☐	☐	☐	☐	☐	

	Rating					
		Excellent			Poor	
Yes/No/N/A	1	2	3	4	5	Comment

Does the report on the audit
committee's activities provide sufficient
detail to enable shareholders to
understand how the audit committee
has discharged its duties? □ □ □ □ □

Does the chairman of the Remuneration
Committee attend the AGM and, where
necessary, answer questions on matters
within the scope of Remuneration
Committee's responsibilities? □ □ □ □ □

Recommendations for improvement

How can the committee improve its performance?

....

....

....

....

....

....

Appendix 8
Guidance on Remuneration Report Disclosures

We have provided a few suggested enhancements to disclosures contained within the remuneration report. These aim to meet the increasing demands for better disclosure from institutional investors and provide an opportunity to demonstrate how the committee is applying its judgement to the various issues contained within the report.

Policy

A key issue here is to provide upper quartile reward for upper quartile performance, but how do you define such performance? Clearly a fundamental factor will be the selection of the peer group and it stands to reason that the chosen peer group and its constituents should not be such that they will be seen by shareholders as an attempt to ratchet up pay levels.

Companies should therefore consider disclosing such peer groups and their constituents in the interests of transparency (see also 'salary' below).

Salary

Investors may want to determine the appropriateness of the peer group used for benchmarking base salaries, so companies should consider disclosing the relevant details, including the constituents, and provide a rationale of why they chose them.

Bonus

Companies should consider disclosing previous years' annual bonus targets and reconcile performance against those targets with the bonuses paid.

Incentive schemes

Investors no longer support retesting of performance criteria and will vote against the Remuneration Report. Where retesting is still a feature companies should provide a clear justification for its use.

Service contracts

Whilst the Directors' Remuneration Report Regulations require disclosure regarding service contracts, it seems fair to say that such disclosure remains relatively opaque. Companies might consider providing greater clarity around the termination payments of executive contracts. Such details could include whether the company would pursue mitigation or phased payments, and a calculation of the final amount to be paid.

Pensions

In light of the future impact of the lifetime allowance on approved pensions, investors are looking for a statement to be included which details the company's current positioning. Institutional investors do not believe that companies should compensate the individual directors for what they see as 'changes to personal tax liabilities'. This has been interpreted to mean that companies should not provide executives with an alternative to pension which has a greater cost to the company than the pension benefit previously provided, although within this there is a wide degree of variation of approach.

To date, few companies have disclosed the course of action they are going to take in light of the forthcoming legislative changes. A greater number have indicated that this is currently under review. Some of those that have disclosed a proposed course of action are looking to implement a cost neutral solution in the form of a cash allowance in lieu of current pension provisions.

Shareholding guidelines

Given the recent trend towards implementing mandatory shareholding guidelines companies ought to include a statement regarding their policy. Details of how the shares are to be sourced (i.e. from incentive schemes), rate of accumulation and over what time period, should also be included.

Companies might also include an analysis of the basis of calculation (i.e. what happens when the share price halves, or doubles?), the precise moment of measurement and whether there is any flexibility to take into account the personal circumstances of each executive.

Other issues

Table on dilution limits

To assist analysts who want to determine the amount of outstanding shares, and therefore the amount of headroom available under the share schemes, companies might want to include a table of dilution limits within the Remuneration Report itself, rather than in the notes to the accounts.

Appendix 9
Suggested benchmarking process (overview of methodology)

Reward philosophy

A key factor in corporate success is people. Companies must ensure that they have the right calibre of people to ensure corporate success and to enhance shareholder value.

Therefore, each company must ensure that its remuneration arrangements are effective in:

- attracting and retaining key employees;

- increasing productivity and profitability;

- encouraging and motivating involvement;

- focusing attention on the achievement of desired goals and objectives.

In setting pay levels it is critical to undertake an independent appraisal of current practices.

Executive compensation packages typically comprise the following components:

- base salary;

- annual incentive programmes;

- long-term incentive plans;

- supplemental benefits.

KPMG Benchmarking Process

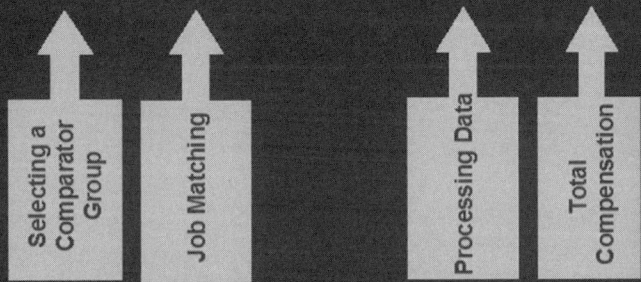

Selecting a Comparator Group

Select a group of similar companies - the 'Comparator Group'. This should comprise of similar companies chosen for their size, business activity and geographic spread
The outcome is a group of at least 10 appropriate companies

Job Matching

Within the Comparator Group, identify comparable main board positions by matching roles
Two methods of benchmarking are used: - benchmarking of actual packages and benchmarking of policy. Benchmarking of policy illustrate packages at target and superior performance levels using the following assumptions:

Level of Performance	Target Performance	Superior Performance
Share Price Growth	Average cost of equity	2 x Average cost of equity
Performance Conditions	Target level vesting	Full vesting
Time to vesting	3 years under all plans	3 years under all plans

Processing Data

Data is aged to bring it up to an estimated market level. Pay is annualised for any executives not serving in the same position throughout the reported year

Total Compensation

Total Compensation benchmarking of Actual packages includes (Base Salary, Annual Bonus, DAB, Options and LTIP). Total Compensation benchmarking of Policy at target (Base Salary, Target Bonus, Target DAB, Target Options and Target LTIP) and superior performance (Base Salary, Max Annual Bonus, Max DAB, Max Options and Max LTIP).

Selecting a comparator group

Selection criteria	Measure	Definition
Size	Market capitalisation	Market capitalisation of the Comparator Group companies should be in the range of 50% to 200% of the client's capitalisation measured on the same basis. The range is chosen as a guideline and should ensure that companies of comparable market capitalisation are included in the Comparator Group.
	Turnover	Turnover (i.e. total annual sales or revenue) of the Comparator Group companies should be 50% to 200% of the client's most recently published figure (i.e. not a forecast).
	Enterprise value	Enterprise value is used as a proxy for the takeover value of a company. It is defined as the sum of market capitalisation, preferred equity, and short and long-term interest-bearing debt, less cash and cash equivalents. For the purpose of Comparator Group selection, enterprise value figure is averaged over a one-year period. The enterprise value of the Comparator Group companies should be 50% to 200% of the client's figure, measured on the same basis.

Selection criteria	Measure	Definition
	Employees	Average number of full-time equivalent employees during the reported year, as disclosed in the most recently published Annual Report and Accounts
Business Activity	Business sector	Every company has a sector classification which includes companies with similar business activities. In most cases, appropriate Comparator Group companies will be in the same sector (determined by the FTSE sector and industry classification)
	Business design and life cycle stage	Business design relates to company strategic goals, strategy of profitability etc. Life cycle stage is the stage of evolution at which a business is at present (e.g. growth, maturity).
Geographic Spread	Percentage of operations (assets, employees etc. oversees)	Geographic spread is the proportion of operations that are located within various geographies. These are mainly measured in terms of proportion of assets or employees in the various geographical locations.

Job matching

Issue	Methodology	Notes
Method matching	Role matching – matching of positions reflecting similar roles within the organisation	The role reflects the 'job' of the individual, determined by factors such as responsibilities, reporting lines, seniority and function.
Classification of roles	For benchmarking of executive director roles the following classification is applied: Chairman – full-time executive chairman Chief Executive – including combined CEO and Chairman Finance Director - most senior finance position. May be titled 'CFO' or 'VP Finance' Other directors – when possible, broken down to: Functional Directors – responsible for a distinct function such as Marketing, Sales, HR, Legal etc Divisional Directors – responsible for a division or business sector such as a geographic area or a line of business.	The classification seeks to group positions that are similar whilst differentiating those that are not. An individual is matched to the role that best describes the job of that individual, typically where most time is spent.

Total compensation

Element	Notes
Base salary	Base salaries are typically obtained from the latest annual report and accounts. These represent the cash value of the executives salary for the reported year.
Annual bonus	Actual bonuses paid are as disclosed in the latest annual reports and accounts, excluding joining and leaving bonuses. Maximum annual bonuses used in the policy analysis are as disclosed in annual reports. When not disclosed, the highest figure in the last 3 years was used. Target levels used in the policy analysis are as disclosed in annual reports or, if not disclosed, assumed to be 50% of the maximum level stated.
Deferred annual bonus	Where the deferral is voluntary, we assume that executives make the maximum deferral allowed under the rules of the plan. When benchmarking actual reward, equity based awards, including matching awards, the binomial model is used for valuation purposes. Valuations are discounted for performance conditions.
Long-term incentives	All grants made under executive plans (i.e. excluding all-employee plans such as SAYE and SIP) are included. When benchmarking actual reward, grants are valued using the binomial model. Valuations are discounted for performance conditions.

Appendix 10
Remuneration Committee Reference Manual

As the Company Secretary should be providing material for the Remuneration Committee meeting, we would suggest that they provide a reference manual for the members of the committee containing key information to enable them to evaluate the relevant issues.

The contents of the manual should be as follows:

1. Remuneration Committee **terms of reference**.

2. Remuneration Committee **agenda and timetable**.

3. Copy of **Remuneration Committee minutes** over last [year].

4. Copy of **Remuneration Report** from latest annual report & accounts.

5. Copy of **plan rules** (including any amendments) for each incentive arrangement (short and long-term).

6. Copy of **trust deed** (including any amendments).

7. Copy of **service contract** for CEO and each main executive director.

8. Summary of **remuneration award/payment history/trends** (e.g. salary increases, annual bonus payments, and long-term incentive grants over last [five years] by individual executive).

9. Summary of each executive's current **individual shareholdings**.

10. Summary of current **dilution and costing** of all remuneration arrangements.

11. Copy of **award certificate and performance condition** for last [three] incentive awards

12. Copy of **participant guide/explanatory booklet** for each incentive arrangement.

13. Remuneration Committee appointed advisers **engagement letter** (including selection criteria and terms of reference)

14. HR/Company Secretarial team **contact details**.

Appendix 11
Recommendations within the Combined Code and Checklist

The following pages detail the principles and provisions of the Combined Code. A checklist is also provided which will allow the Remuneration Committee to check the level of compliance or non-compliance with the Code. Pinpointing areas of non-compliance will either allow for remedial action to be taken or for specific disclosure and explanation to be given for the non-compliance within the Remuneration Report. The Code provisions that are most directly relevant to the Remuneration Committee are indicated by the [•] symbol. Those that relate to the shareholder relations function are also indicated.

Source: UK Combined Code Provisions	Reference	Board	Company X		
			Appointments and Nomination Committee	Remuneration Policy and Remuneration Committee	Shareholder Relations
Principles					
Every company should be headed by an effective board.	CC A.1	•			
Board's role is to provide entrepreneurial leadership, set strategic aims and company values and standards and ensure shareholder obligations are met and sufficient resources in place to meet its objectives and review management performance.	CC A.1	•			
Directors must take decisions objectively in company's interests.	CC A.1	•			
NEDs should constructively challenge and help develop strategy, scrutinise performance, monitor financial systems and information, determine executive remuneration and have a prime role in appointing/employing directors.	CC A.1	•			
Provisions					
Board should meet regularly with a formal schedule.	CC A.1.1.	•			
Annual report should include statements on how the board operates, including a statement on which decisions are taken by the board and which are delegated to management.	CC A.1.1.	•			

Source: UK Combined Code Provisions	Reference	Board	Company X Appointments and Nomination Committee	Company X Remuneration Policy and Remuneration Committee	Company X Shareholder Relations
Annual report should identify chairman, deputy, CEO, SID, NEDs, committee members, number of meetings of board and committees and individual attendance for each.	CC A.1.2.	•			
Chairman should hold meetings with NEDs without the executives present and NEDs should meet without chairman at least once to appraise chairman's performance.	CC A.1.3	•			
Where directors have unresolved concerns on running the business these should be minuted. On resignation, NED should cover such concerns in a written statement to the chairman.	CC A.1.4	•			
Company should arrange appropriate insurance cover for directors against legal action.	CC A.1.5	•			
Principles					
Should be clear division of responsibility at the head of company between running of the board and the executive responsibility for running the business, ensuring directors receive accurate, timely and clear information.	CC A.2	•			

Source: UK Combined Code Provisions	Reference	Company X			
		Board	Appointments and Nomination Committee	Remuneration Policy and Remuneration Committee	Shareholder Relations
No individual should have unvetted powers of decision.		•			
Chairman is responsible for board leadership, ensuring its effectiveness and setting its agenda; chairman should facilitate the effective contribution of NEDs and ensure constructive and effective communication with shareholders.	CC A.2	•			
Provisions					
Roles of chairman and CEO should be separate with division of responsibilities written down and agreed by board.	CC A.2.1	•			
On appointment chairman should be independent.	CC A.2.2	•			
CEO should not go on to be chairman of same company; if exception board should consult major shareholders in advance and give reason on appointment and in annual report.	CC A.2.2	•			
Principles					
Board should be a balance of executives and NEDs so no individual or group dominates decision-making.	CC A.3	•			

Source: UK Combined Code Provisions	Reference	Board	Company X		
			Appointments and Nomination Committee	Remuneration Policy and Remuneration Committee	Shareholder Relations
Board should be of sufficient size so it has an appropriate balance of skills and experience and changes can be managed without disruption; the value of refreshing committee membership should be taken into account and there should be no undue reliance on particular individuals; no one other than members of committees is entitled to attend committee meetings, except by invitation.	CC A.3	•			
Provisions					
Board should identify in annual report each NED it considers to be independent in character and judgement (provision includes further explanation of independence) and whether there are relationship circumstances which could affect judgement.	CC A.3.1	•			
At least half the board should be independent NEDs (or for smaller companies, i.e. those below FTSE350 throughout prior year, only two).	CC A.3.2	•			
Board should appoint independent NED as SID who should be available to shareholders if normal channels are ineffective/inappropriate.	CC A.3.2	•			

Source: UK Combined Code Provisions	Reference	Company X			
		Board	Appointments and Nomination Committee	Remuneration Policy and Remuneration Committee	Shareholder Relations
Principles					
Should be formal, rigorous and transparent appointment procedure for new board appointments.	CC A.4	•			
Appointments should be made on merit against objective criteria; appointees must have enough time for job (especially chairman); board should ensure orderly succession plans in place for board and senior management to maintain balance of skills and experience.	CC A.4	•			
Provisions					
Nomination committee should lead board appointment process and make recommendations.	CC A.4.1		•		
Majority of members should be independent NEDs; the company chairman or an independent NED should chair committee. Chairman should not chair when considering appointment of successor chairman.	CC A.4.1		•		
Nomination committee should make terms of reference available, explaining role and delegated authority (satisfied by making it available on request and on website).	CC A.4.1		•		

Source: UK Combined Code Provisions	Reference	Board	Company X		
			Appointments and Nomination Committee	Remuneration Policy and Remuneration Committee	Shareholder Relations
Nomination committee should evaluate balance of skills, knowledge and experience and prepare role and capabilities description.	CC A.4.2		•		
For chairman appointment, nomination committee should prepare job specification, including time commitment. Chairman's other commitments should be disclosed to board before appointment and disclosed in annual report. Changes should be reported to board and disclosed in the annual report accounts. No individual should be appointed a second FTSE100 chairmanship.	CC A.4.3		•		
NED terms of appointment should be available for inspection. Letter of appointment should include time commitment. Significant other commitments including time involved should be disclosed to board before appointment and updated for changes.	CC A.4.4		•		
Board should not agree to executive director taking on more than one FTSE100 NED position or a FTSE100 chairmanship position.	CC A.4.5		•		

Source: UK Combined Code Provisions	Reference	Company X			
		Board	Appointments and Nomination Committee	Remuneration Policy and Remuneration Committee	Shareholder Relations
Separate section of report should describe work of nomination committee, including board appointment process and reasons if search consultancies and open advertising have not been issued.	CC A.4.6		•		
Principles					
Board should be supplied with timely information of appropriate quality to discharge its duties. All directors should receive induction and regularly update their skills and knowledge.	CC A.5	•			
Chairman, assisted by company secretary are responsible for ensuring directors receive accurate, timely and clear information from management, update skills and company familiarity to fulfil role. Company should provide necessary resources. Company Secretary should be responsible for ad using the board, through the chairman on all governance matters.	CC A.5	•			

Source: UK Combined Code Provisions	Reference	Board	Company X		
			Appointments and Nomination Committee	Remuneration Policy and Remuneration Committee	Shareholder Relations
Provisions					
Chairman should ensure new directors receive full, formal and tailored induction and major shareholders offered opportunity to meet new NEDs.	CC A.5.1	•			
Board should ensure all directors have access to independent professional advice and advice/services of company secretary. Committees should have sufficient resources to undertake their duties. Company Secretary responsible to the board for ensuring board procedures complied with.	CC A.5.2 and 3	•			
Appointment and removal of company secretary is matter for board.	CC A.5.3	•			
Principles					
Board should undertake formal and rigorous annual evaluation of own performance, that of committees and individuals.	CC A.6	•			
Individual evaluation should aim to show continued effective contribution and commitment. Chairman should act on results and where appropriate propose new members/seek directors' resignation.	CC A.6	•			

Source: UK Combined Code Provisions	Reference	Board	Company X Appointments and Nomination Committee	Remuneration Policy and Remuneration Committee	Shareholder Relations
Provisions					
Board should state in annual report how performance evaluation of board committees and individual directors has been conducted.	CC A.6.1	•			
NEDs led by SID should be responsible for chairman's evaluation, taking into account the views of executive directors.	CC A.6.1	•			
Principles					
All directors should be subject to regular re-election, subject to satisfactory performance. There should be planned and progressive refreshing of the board.	CC A.7	•			
Provisions					
All directors should be subject to re-election at first AGM after appointment and thereafter at no more than 3 yr intervals. Shareholders should have sufficient details to make informed decision.	CC A.7.1	•			

| Source: UK Combined Code Provisions | Reference | Company X | | | |
		Board	Appointments and Nomination Committee	Remuneration Policy and Remuneration Committee	Shareholder Relations
NEDs should be appointed for specified terms subject to reflection and cost provisions. In papers accompanying election resolution, board should set out reasons why NED should be elected. Chairman should confirm director's commitment and effective performance.	CC A.7.2	•			
Any term beyond 6 yrs should be subject to rigorous review and beyond 9 subject to annual re-election any which may impact on independence.	CC A.7.2	•			
Principles					
Remuneration levels should be sufficient to attract, retain and motivate. A significant proportion should be performance-linked (corporate and individual).	CC B.1			•	
Remuneration Committee should judge where to position company relative to others but with caution to avoid ratcheting; should be sensitive to pay and conditions elsewhere in group.	CC B.1			•	

Source: UK Combined Code Provisions	Reference	Company X			
		Board	Appointments and Nomination Committee	Remuneration Policy and Remuneration Committee	Shareholder Relations
Provisions					
Performance-related remuneration should be significant, aligned with shareholders' interests and give incentives for highest performance.	CC B.1.2			•	
Remuneration Committee should follow Schedule A of Code (see below).	CC B.1.2			•	
Remuneration Committee should consider if executive directors should be eligible for bonuses.	Schedule A			•	
Bonus performance conditions should be relevant, stretching and enhance shareholder value.	Schedule A			•	
Bonus upper limits should be set and disclosed and there may be a case for part payment in shares to be held.	Schedule A			•	
Remuneration Committee should consider if executive directors should be eligible for LTIs.	Schedule A			•	
The use of options should be weighted against other LTI schemes.	Schedule A			•	

Source: UK Combined Code Provisions	Reference	Board	Appointments and Nomination Committee	Remuneration Policy and Remuneration Committee	Shareholder Relations
				Company X	
Share awards, deferred compensation and options should not vest in less than 3 years.	Schedule A			•	
Directors should be encouraged to hold shares for further period after vesting, subject to financing related costs.	Schedule A			•	
Any new LTI plan should be approved by shareholders as part of well considered overall plan. Potential total rewards should not be excessive.	Schedule A			•	
All incentive based payments/grants should be subject to challenging performance criteria reflecting the company's objectives. Consider criteria that reflects relative performance e.g. TSR.	Schedule A			•	
Option and LTI grants should be phased.	Schedule A			•	
Only basic salary should be pensionable.	Schedule A			•	
Remuneration Committee should consider impact on pension of salary increases and other changes.	Schedule A			•	

Source: UK Combined Code Provisions	Reference	Company X			
		Board	Appointments and Nomination Committee	Remuneration Policy and Remuneration Committee	Shareholder Relations
Provisions					
Executive options should not normally be offered at a discount.	CC B.1.2			●	
NED remuneration should reflect time commitment and responsibility, and should not normally include share options. If options are granted, shareholder approval should be sought in advance and shares held for 1 year after leaving the board.	CC B.1.3			●	
Remuneration report should include statement on whether executive directors retain any non-executive earnings and the amounts.	CC B.1.4			●	
Remuneration Committee should carefully consider early termination provisions, avoid rewarding poor performance and take robust line on mitigation.	CC B.1.5			●	
Notice periods should be set at one year or less (longer periods for new hires should reduce to 1 year or less as early as possible).	CC B.1.6			●	

Source: UK Combined Code Provisions	Reference	Company X			
		Board	Appointments and Nomination Committee	Remuneration Policy and Remuneration Committee	Shareholder Relations
Principles					
Should be formal and transparent process for developing executive remuneration policy and fixing packages with no director involved with decision on own pay.	CC B.2			•	
Remuneration Committee should consult chairman/CEO on remuneration proposals of other executive directors.	CC B.2			•	
Remuneration Committee should be responsible for appointing external consultants on executive directors' pay.	CC B.3			•	
With internal advisors, Remuneration Committee should recognise and avoid conflicts of interest.	CC B.4			•	
Company chairman should ensure contact with shareholders on remuneration in same way as for other matters.	CC B.5			•	
Provisions					
Remuneration Committee should consist of at least 3 independent NEDs (2 for smaller companies).	CC B.2.1			•	

Source: UK Combined Code Provisions	Reference	Company X			
		Board	Appointments and Nomination Committee	Remuneration Policy and Remuneration Committee	Shareholder Relations
Remuneration Committee should make terms of reference available on role and delegated authority and make statement on whether remuneration consultants have other connection with company.	CC B.2.1			•	
Remuneration Committee should have delegated responsibility for setting chairman's remuneration.	CC B.2.2			•	
Remuneration Committee should recommend and monitor senior management remuneration ('senior management' defined by board but should normally include first layer of management below the board).	CC B.2.2			•	
Board (shareholders or committee with CEO) as permitted by the Articles of Association should determine NED remuneration	CC B.2.3			•	
Shareholders should approve all new LTIs and ensure reliance with the Listing Rules.	CC B.2.4			•	
Principles					
There should be an ongoing dialogue with shareholders based on mutual understanding, with board as whole taking responsibility for satisfactory dialogue.	CC D.1				•

Source: UK Combined Code Provisions	Reference	Board	Company X		
			Appointments and Nomination Committee	Remuneration Policy and Remuneration Committee	Shareholder Relations
Most shareholder contact is with CEO and FD, but chairman should maintain sufficient contact to understand their issues and concerns.	CC D.1				•
Provisions					
Chairman should ensure shareholder views communicated to board. Chairman should discuss strategy and governance with major shareholders.	CC D.1.1				•
NEDs should be offered opportunity to attend meetings called by major shareholder. SID should attend sufficient meetings to understand their issues and concerns.	CC D.1.1				•
Board should state in annual report steps taken to ensure board members have understanding of major shareholders' views (e.g. face-to-face contact, analyst/brokers briefing, surveys of shareholder opinion).	CC D.1.2				•
Principles					
Board should use AGM to communicate with investors and encourage their participation.	CC D.2				•

Source: UK Combined Code Provisions	Reference	Company X			
		Board	Appointments and Nomination Committee	Remuneration Policy and Remuneration Committee	Shareholder Relations
Provisions					
Company should count all proxies, indicate level of proxies and balance for/against and abstentions. Company should ensure votes cast are properly received and recorded.	CC D.2.1				•
Company should propose resolution for each substantially separate issue (including reports and accounts).	CC D.2.2				•
Chairman should arrange for all directors to attend and committee chairmen to answer questions.	CC D.2.3				•
Company should arrange for AGM notice and papers to be sent at least 20 days in advance.	CC D.2.4				•

Appendix 12
ABI Guidelines and Checklist

The ABI Guidelines on remuneration were reviewed and updated in December 2005. The checklist will enable the Remuneration Committee to check for non-compliance with the provisions. While the ABI does not provide voting recommendations to its members, it does signal breaches of the provisions.

Source: ABI Remuneration Principles and Guidelines and Share Incentive Scheme Guidelines	Reference	Board	Company X		
			Appointments and Nomination Committee	Remuneration Policy and Remuneration Committee	Shareholder Relations
Remuneration Committee should maintain dialogue with shareholders and ABI on remuneration. Any proposed departure from the stated remuneration policy should be subject to prior approval by shareholders.	Principle 1			•	
Remuneration Committee should be properly established, with appropriate powers of authority delegated by board.	Principle 2			•	
Boards should demonstrate performance-related pay aligned to business strategy and objectives and ensure that overall arrangements are prudent, well communicated, incentivise effectively and recognise shareholder expectations.	Principle 3	•		•	
Variable and share-based remuneration should not be payable unless performance conditions used are robust. Remuneration Committees should work with Audit Committees in evaluating performance criteria.	Principle 4			•	
Remuneration Committees should consider pay and conditions elsewhere in the group and demonstrate that appropriate analysis supports the level of remuneration. External comparisons must be used with caution.	Principle 5			•	

Source: ABI Remuneration Principles and Guidelines and Share Incentive Scheme Guidelines	Reference	Company X			
		Board	Appointments and Nomination Committee	Remuneration Policy and Remuneration Committee	Shareholder Relations
Remuneration Committees should consider remuneration arrangements for key senior executives who are not board members.	Principle 6			•	
New share-based plans should be subject to shareholder approval. Where there is flexibility on levels and performance criteria, any changes should be disclosed in remuneration report. Any substantial changes in operation should be subject to prior shareholder approval.	Principle 7			•	•
There should be separate shareholder votes on performance-linked enhancement or matching shares in respect of deferred bonus arrangements.	Principle 8			•	•
There should be transparency on remuneration arrangements of current and past directors, and where appropriate other senior executives. Shareholders' attention should be drawn to special arrangements and significant changes from the last report.	Principle 9			•	•

Source: ABI Remuneration Principles and Guidelines and Share Incentive Scheme Guidelines	Reference	Company X			
		Board	Appointments and Nomination Committee	Remuneration Policy and Remuneration Committee	Shareholder Relations
Remuneration should be within the scope of the policy approved by shareholders. Where, in exceptional circumstances, there has been provision for remuneration beyond this scope, relevant details must be disclosed and justified.	Principle 10			•	•
Shareholders consider it inapproprite for chairmen and independent directors to be in receipt of incentive awards geared to the share price or performance, as this could impair their ability to provide impartial oversight and advice	Principle 11			•	•
Awards should be structure to promote as close as possible an alignment of participants with the risks and rewards faced by shareholders. It is undesirable for directors to seek out leveraged arrangements on the price of the company's securities.	Principle 12			•	•
Package should be balanced between fixed and variable and STIs and LTIs.	Guideline 1			•	
For salaries, Remuneration Committee should consider market. Remuneration Committee should be able to satisfy shareholders that the company is not paying more than necessary to attract and retain directors.	Guideline 2			•	•

Source: ABI Remuneration Principles and Guidelines and Share Incentive Scheme Guidelines	Reference	Company X			
		Board	Appointments and Nomination Committee	Remuneration Policy and Remuneration Committee	Shareholder Relations
Setting salary below median provides more scope for increasing variable pay.	Guideline 3			•	
Annual bonuses provide useful means of short-term incentivisation, but should be performance-related. Both individual and corporate targets are relevant. Review regularly.	Guideline 4			•	
Where short-term targets are not disclosed because of commercial confidentiality shareholders expect to be informed about the main performance parameters, both corporate and personal, adopted in the financial year being reported on. Maximum participation levels should be disclosed and annual bonuses should not be pensionable.	Guideline 5			•	
Remuneration Committees are responsible for ensuring that targets set out in bonus arrangements have been properly fulfilled. They should work with the Audit Committee to ensure that the basis for their decision is correct	Guideline 6			•	
Any material payments that may be viewed as being ex-gratia in nature should be fully explained, justified and subject to shareholder approval prior to payment. Shareholders are not supportive of transaction bonuses.	Guideline 7			•	•

Source: ABI Remuneration Principles and Guidelines and Share Incentive Scheme Guidelines	Reference	Company X			
		Board	Appointments and Nomination Committee	Remuneration Policy and Remuneration Committee	Shareholder Relations
The board should regularly review the potential board liabilities associated with all elements of remuneration and make appropriate disclosures to shareholders.	Guideline 8	•		•	•
There should be informative disclosure identifying incremental value accruing to pension scheme participation and any other superannuation arrangements and related contingent commitments, during year .	Guideline 9			•	
Changes to transfer values should be fully explained. Discretionary increases in pension entitlement, significant changes in actuarial and other relevant assumptions and ex-gratia awards or contributions should be fully explained and justified.	Guideline 9			•	
Re changes to pensions taxation, companies are not responsible for compensating individuals for a change in personal tax liabilities. The extent to which actual and potential liabilities such as pension promises or early retirement benefits are funded should be disclosed, together with any aggregate outstanding unfunded liabilities.	Guideline 10			•	

Source: ABI Remuneration Principles and Guidelines and Share Incentive Scheme Guidelines	Reference	Company X			
		Board	Appointments and Nomination Committee	Remuneration Policy and Remuneration Committee	Shareholder Relations
Remuneration Committees should scrutinise all other benefits to ensure that they are justified and disclosed.	Guideline 11			•	
Remuneration Committees should be aware of outstanding dilution in accordance with the Guideline limits and where appropriate available dilution capacity should be disclosed.	Guideline 12			•	
In line with encouraging senior executives to build meaningful shareholders in companies, remuneration committees should consider incorporating provisions in the rules of incentive schemes to require retention of a proportion of shares until such times as shareholding guidelines are met.	Guideline 13			•	
The Chairman and non-executive directors should be appropriately remunerated either in cash or in shares. If share incentives are granted to Chairman these should be fully discussed and approved by shareholders in advance.	Guideline 14			•	•
Generally support schemes linked to performance for exec directors and senior executive.	Guideline 1.1			•	
Schemes should be objectively costed, well-designed and a coherent part of package.	Guideline 1.2			•	

Source: ABI Remuneration Principles and Guidelines and Share Incentive Scheme Guidelines	Reference	Company X			
		Board	Appointments and Nomination Committee	Remuneration Policy and Remuneration Committee	Shareholder Relations
Guidelines apply to all share-based schemes, including arrangements for option gains to be settled in shares or cash.	Guideline 1.3			•	
Share incentive schemes should follow the spirit of the Guidelines.	Guideline 1.4			•	
Schemes should emphasise performance link, dilution limits, individual participation, shareholder alignment, with regard to costs, which should be disclosed.	Guideline 2.1			•	
Strongly encourage phased grants and sliding scales.	Guideline 2.2			•	
Dilution under all schemes should not exceed 10% in any 10-year period, with further limitations of 5% in 10 years on discretionary schemes.	Guideline 2.3			•	
Guidelines should apply to all share incentive schemes or arrangements sponsored by UK listed companies.	Guideline 3.1			•	
Remuneration Committees should regularly review schemes, to ensure effectiveness, compliance and contribution to shareholder value.	Guideline 4.1			•	

Source: ABI Remuneration Principles and Guidelines and Share Incentive Scheme Guidelines	Reference	Board	Appointments and Nomination Committee	Company X – Remuneration Policy and Remuneration Committee	Shareholder Relations
Remuneration Committees should disclose in the remuneration report as to whether a review of the current share incentive schemes has been undertaken to ensure they remain appropriate to the company's current circumstances and prospects.	Guideline 4.1			•	
Remuneration Committees should obtain prior approval for substantive or exceptional amendments to scheme rules and practice.	Guideline 4.1			•	
Companies should make full disclosure in remuneration report and in new proposals regarding share schemes and their rationale.	Guideline 5.1			•	
Scheme and individual limits should be disclosed. Disclosure should cover performance conditions, costs, dilution limits and reasons for performance conditions.	Guideline 5.2			•	
Vesting of awards should be conditional on satisfaction of performance criteria and demonstrate demanding and stretching financial performance.	Guideline 6.1			•	

Source: ABI Remuneration Principles and Guidelines and Share Incentive Scheme Guidelines	Reference	Company X			
		Board	Appointments and Nomination Committee	Remuneration Policy and Remuneration Committee	Shareholder Relations
Performance conditions should relate to overall performance; demonstrate demanding achievement; measured relative to a defined peer group or benchmark and be disclosed and transparent.	Guideline 6.2			•	
Threshold vesting levels should not be significant by comparison to annual salary. Award structures with "cliff-edge" vesting profiles are inappropriate.	Guideline 6.3			•	
The greater the level of reward, the more stretching and demanding performance conditions should be. Full vesting should be significantly greater value creation than that applicable to threshold vesting and there should be clear explanation as to how this is achieved.	Guideline 6.4			•	
Sliding scales are generally preferable to single hurdle.	Guideline 6.5			•	
Further performance conditions should apply to annual bonus share match.	Guideline 6.6			•	
All types of performance conditions should be fully explained.	Guideline 7.1			•	

			Company X			
Source: ABI Remuneration Principles and Guidelines and Share Incentive Scheme Guidelines	Reference	Board	Appointments and Nomination Committee	Remuneration Policy and Remuneration Committee	Shareholder Relations
Comparator groups must be relevant and representative. If a comparator group is small in number the Remuneration Committee must ensure that there are no arbitary outcomes inconsistent with the Guidelines. Awards should not be made for less than median performance	Guideline 7.2			•	
TSR relevant to index/peer group is one of a number of generally acceptable performance criteria. The Remuneration Committee should satisfy itself prior to vesting that the recorded TSR or other criterion is a genuine reflection of underlying financial performance.	Guideline 7.3			•	
Where TSR is used and the comparator group contains some overseas companies, it is essential that TSR be measured on a consistent basis. A standard approach is to use common currency and companies should provide full explanation where this approach is not used.	Guideline 7.4			•	
Remuneration Committees should be careful to ensure that the definition of earnings per share (EPS) or any other financial measure that they may employ will fully reflect performance of the business on a consistent basis in respect of the measurement period.	Guideline 7.5			•	

			Company X		
Source: ABI Remuneration Principles and Guidelines and Share Incentive Scheme Guidelines	Reference	Board	Appointments and Nomination Committee	Remuneration Policy and Remuneration Committee	Shareholder Relations
Maximum grant levels should be disclosed.	Guideline 7.6			•	
Premium exercise price is not normally a substitute for performance conditions.	Guideline 7.7			•	
Re-testing is unnecessary and unjustified. The stipulated performance conditions should never combined a fixed performance hurdle with measurement from a variable base date.	Guideline 8.1			•	
Performance conditions should be measured over 3 or more years. Strong encouragement given to periods of more than 3 years.	Guideline 9.1			•	
Remuneration Committees should also be mindful that the size of the grants made on this basis takes into account reasonable expectations as to the value of the dividend stream on the company's shares over the period to vesting.	Guideline 9.2			•	

Source: ABI Remuneration Principles and Guidelines and Share Incentive Scheme Guidelines	Reference	Company X			
		Board	Appointments and Nomination Committee	Remuneration Policy and Remuneration Committee	Shareholder Relations
Remuneration Committees may apply conditions to grant rather than vesting but only in exceptional circumstances, for example if (a) executives are exposed to global remuneration practices, and (b) conditions at grant relate to corporate performance, or (c) it is disclosed and explain (d) minimum 3 yr exercise period and dilution limits met, and (e) participants build up significant shareholding.	Guideline 10.1			•	
Rules should state no automatic waiving of performance conditions on (a) change in control, (b) roll over and (c) early termination	Guideline 11.1			•	
Shareholders expect underlying financial performance of a company subject to change of control should be a key determinant of what share-based awards should vest.	Guideline 11.2			•	•
In the event of change of control awards should vest on a pro-rata basis.	Guideline 11.3			•	
Cost of schemes should be disclosed at time of approval (cost of all incentives; potential value on full vesting (based on face value); expected value; max dilution).	Guideline 11.1			•	

Source: ABI Remuneration Principles and Guidelines and Share Incentive Scheme Guidelines	Reference	Company X			
		Board	Appointments and Nomination Committee	Remuneration Policy and Remuneration Committee	Shareholder Relations
There should be prudent and appropriate arrangements for share purchases to meet scheme obligations.	Guideline 11.2			•	
Comprehensive approach to valuation, with focus on expected value (EV), taking account of vesting schedule and retesting. Disclosure of EV and face value (FV).	Guideline 11.3			•	
Dilution limit of 10% in any 10 yr rolling period for issue of new shares or utilisation of treasury shares under all schemes. Remuneration Committee should ensure flow rate policies exist.	Guideline 20.1			•	
Dilution limit of 5% over 10 yrs for issue of new shares or treasury shares for executive (discretionary) schemes. This may be exceeded where vesting is dependent on stretching performance criteria.	Guideline 20.2			•	
The implicit dilution commitment should always be provided for at point of grant even where, as in the case of share-settled share appreciation rights, it is recognised that only a proportion of shares may in practice be used.	Guideline 20.3			•	

Source: ABI Remuneration Principles and Guidelines and Share Incentive Scheme Guidelines	Reference	Company X			
		Board	Appointments and Nomination Committee	Remuneration Policy and Remuneration Committee	Shareholder Relations
For small companies, up to 10% of the ordinary share capital may be utilised for executive (discretionary) schemes, provided that the total market value of the capital utilised for the scheme at the time of grant does not exceed £500,000.	Guideline 20.4			•	
Participation in share incentive schemes should be restricted to bona fide employees and directors with disclosed individual participation limits.	Guideline 13.1			•	
Grant policy should be disclosed and consistently applied. In the event of falling share price, it is important to avoid unjustified increases in number of shares or options awarded.	Guideline 13.2			•	
Participation in more than one scheme should be part of well-considered remuneration policy, not to raise pay out prospects.	Guideline 13.3			•	
Shareholders are not supportive of shares/options granted at a discount.	Guideline 13.4			•	•

Source: ABI Remuneration Principles and Guidelines and Share Incentive Scheme Guidelines	Reference	Company X			
		Board	Appointments and Nomination Committee	Remuneration Policy and Remuneration Committee	Shareholder Relations
Regular phasing of awards or options grants on annual basis encouraged.	Guideline 14.1			•	
Issue price should not be less than mid-market price immediately preceding grant.	Guideline 15.1			•	
Options granted under executive (discretionary) schemes should not be granted at a discount.	Guideline 15.2			•	
Repricing or surrender and re-grant of awards or underwater options not appropriate.	Guideline 15.3			•	
Scheme rules should provide that awards only made within 42-day period from results publication.	Guideline 16.1			•	
No awards beyond life of scheme, should not exceed 10 yrs.	Guideline 17.1			•	
Shares and options should not vest/ be exercisable within 3 yrs of grant (and options should not be exercisable more than 10 yrs from grant).	Guideline 17.2			•	
Options/conditional awards should be granted in expectation of service over the performance measurement period of not less than 3 years.	Guideline 17.3			•	

Source: ABI Remuneration Principles and Guidelines and Share Incentive Scheme Guidelines	Reference	Company X			
		Board	Appointments and Nomination Committee	Remuneration Policy and Remuneration Committee	Shareholder Relations
Where individuals choose to terminate their employment before the end of the service period, or in the event that employment is terminated for cause, any unvested options or conditional share-based award should normally lapse.	Guideline 17.4			•	
Where the individual is unable to complete the period of service, it is to be expected that some portion of the award will vest, at least to the extent of the service period that has been completed but subject or the achievement of the appropriate performance criteria.	Guideline 17.5			•	
On takeover, death, cessation employment options may be exercised (lapse) within 12 months.	Guideline 17.6			•	
Any shares/options granted on takeover should be taken into account for dilution/individual limit purposes.	Guideline 17.7			•	

Source: ABI Remuneration Principles and Guidelines and Share Incentive Scheme Guidelines	Reference	Board	Appointments and Nomination Committee	Company X — Remuneration Policy and Remuneration Committee	Shareholder Relations
In the event of retirement, treatment of awards should reflect the principle that awards are granted in respect of the year in question and in expectation of service over the performance period of at least 3 years. Where the treatment does not follow that provided for in paragraph 16.5, awards made within 12 months of actual retirement date must be subject to pro-rating in respect of the balance of the 12 month period following grant which falls after the actual date of retirement	Guideline 18.1			•	
In determining the size and other terms of a grant made within 3 years of the anticipated retirement date, Remuneration Committees should have regard to the executive's ability to contribute to the achievement of the performance conditions.	Guideline 18.1			•	
Any unvested options/conditional shares on retirement should be subject to a performance measurement over stipulated period. If early exercise required, performance should be pro-rated. Options should vest by end of initial performance period and be exercisable no later than 12 months.	Guideline 18.2			•	

Source: ABI Remuneration Principles and Guidelines and Share Incentive Scheme Guidelines	Reference	Company X			
		Board	Appointments and Nomination Committee	Remuneration Policy and Remuneration Committee	Shareholder Relations
Generally undesirable to have options over JV shares.	Guideline 19.1			•	
In normal circumstances grants over shares in subsidiary should not be made (with exceptions) such as flotation or sale of subsidiary.	Guideline 19.2			•	
All-employee plans should operate within best practice framework (e.g. dilution limits).	Guideline 22.1			•	
ESOTs should not hold more shares at any one time than would be required in practice to match their outstanding liabilities. Prior shareholder approval should be obtained before 5% or more of share capital held by ESOTs.	Guideline 21.1			•	
The number of shares held by the ESOT should be disclosed to assist shareholders with their evaluation of the overall use of shares for remuneration purposes.	Guideline 21.2			•	•

Directory

This directory contains a list of the contact details of the ABI, NAPF, certain proxy voting agencies and institutional investors. These are the appropriate contacts as of June 2006.

Investor bodies

The ABI and NAPF have produced corporate governance guidelines and should be approached for any discussion on governance, and particularly on issues of non-compliance with the various provisions.

Association of British Insurers (ABI)
51 Gresham Street
London
EC2V 7HQ
Phone: +44 (0)20 7216 7670/7627/7659
www.abi.org.uk

National Association of Pension Funds (NAPF)
NIOC House
4 Victoria Street
London
SW1H 0NX
(*See also* RREV)
Phone: +44 (0)20 7808 1340
www.napf.co.uk

Proxy voting agencies

PIRC, RREV and Manifest provide their clients with an analysis of governance standards at UK companies and provide voting recommendations on the various resolutions at company general meetings.

Manifest
9 Freebournes Court
Newland Street
Witham
Essex
CM8 2BL
Phone: +44 (0)1376 503500
www.manifest.co.uk

Pensions & Investment Research Consultants (PIRC)
4th Floor
Cityside
40 Adler Street
London
E1 1EE
Phone: +44 (0)20 7247 2323 (ext. 230)
www.pirc.co.uk

Research Recommendations and Electronic Voting
Epworth House
25 City Road
London
EC1Y 1AA
(see also NAPF)
Phone: +44 (0)20 7614 8534
www.rrev.co.uk

Institutional investors

The institutional investors listed below feature some of the larger names in the investment management community, but the list is comprehensive in terms of those institutions which are known to play a leading role in the governance debate. Where they appear on a company's shareholder register they can be approached directly on governance issues and should, in the main, be invited to take part in any remuneration consultation.

AXA Investment Managers
7 Newgate Street
London
EC1A 7NX
Phone: +44 (0)20 7003 2105
www.axa-im.com

Baillie Gifford
Calton Square
1 Greenside Row
Edinburgh
EH1 3AN
Phone: +44 (0)131 275 3003
www.bailliegifford.com

Barclays Global Investors
Murray House
1 Royal Mint Court
London
EC3N 4HH
Phone: +44 (0)20 7668 8027
www.barclaysglobal.com

Capital International
40 Grosvenor Place
London
SW1X 7GG
Phone: +44 (0)20 7864 5128
www.capgroup.com

Deutsche Asset Management
One Appold Street
London
EC2A 2UU
Phone: +44 (0)20 7545 0072
www.deam-uk.com/uk/institutional/aboutUs/governance.htm

F&C Asset Management plc
Exchange House
Primrose Street
London
EC2A 2NY
Phone: +44 (0)20 7506 1244
www.fandc.com/aboutus.asp?locale=UK&pageid=1.3

Fidelity Investment Management Ltd
25 Cannon Street
London
EC4M 5TA
Phone: +44 (0)20 7961 4873
www.fidelity.co.uk

Gartmore Investment Management plc
Gartmore House
8 Fenchurch Place
London
EC3M 4PB
Phone: +44 (0)20 7782 2207
www.gartmore.com

Henerson Global Investors
4 Broadgate
London
EC2M 2DA
Phone: +44 (0)20 7818 2163
www.henderson.co.uk/home/uk/governance/corporate_responsibility/

Hermes Pensions Management Ltd
Lloyds Chambers
1 Portsoken Street
London
E1 8HZ
Phone: +44 (0)20 7680 2251
www.hermes.co.uk/corporate_governance/corporate_governance_introduction.htm

Insight Investment
33 Old Broad Street
London
EC2N 1HZ
Phone: +44 (0)20 7321 1040
www.insightinvestment.com

JP Morgan Asset Management
20 Finsbury Street
London
EC2Y 9AQ
Phone: +44 (0)20 7742 5736
www.jpmorgan.com

Leal & General Investment Management Ltd
Bucklersbury House
3 Queen Victoria Street
London
EC4N 8NH
Phone: +44 (0)20 7528 6663
www.lgim.com

M&G Investment Management Ltd
Governor's House
Laurence Pountney Hill
London
EC4R 0HH
Phone: +44 (0)20 7548 3116
www.mandg.co.uk

Morley Fund Management Ltd
No 1 Poultry
London
EC2R 8EJ
Phone: +44 (0)20 7809 8205
www.morleyfm.com/about_morley/corporate_governance/index.htm

Newton
Mellon Financial Centre
160 Queen Victoria Street
London
EC4V 4LA
Phone: +44 (0)20 7163 2022
www.newton.co.uk/institutional/products/segregated/corp_gov_and_custody.html

Schroder Investment Management Limited
31 Gresham Street
London
EC2V 7QA
Phone: +44 (0)20 7658 3991
www.schroders.com

Standard Life Investments
1 George Street
Edinburgh
EH2 2LL
Phone: +44 (0)131 245 6813
www.standardlifeinvestments.com

Investor voting policies and corporate governance: useful websites

UK

Association of British Insurers (ABI)

www.abi.org.uk

Institutional Voting Information Service (IVIS)

www.ivis.co.uk

On this website you can find copies of the guidelines plus the proxy voting documents for all listed companies. You will need a username and password for the proxy voting documents.

National Association of Pension Funds (NAPF)

www.napf.co.uk

RREV (Research Recommendations Electronic Voting)

www.rrev.co.uk

RREV serves the corporate governance and proxy voting needs of UK-based institutional investors. RREV is a joint venture which brings together the National Association of Pension Funds (NAPF), with a long established and leading reputation in UK corporate governance, with Institutional Shareholder Services (ISS), the leading provider of global research and proxy voting services.

Europe

Deminor

www.deminor.org

A Brussels-based consultancy with offices in Amsterdam, Paris, Frankfurt and Rome. They work with both companies and investors to promote higher standards of corporate governance. Recently formed a link with the NAPF to promote shareholder voting throughout Europe. www.deminorrating.com

They have a ratings system which analyses companies' commitment to corporate governance.

The European Corporate Governance Institute

www.ecgi.org

This site provides a forum for debate and dialogue between academics, legislators and practioners, focusing on major corporate governance issues and thereby promoting best practice.

North America

CalPERS (California Public Employees' Retirement System) – US

www.calpers-governance.org/principles/

One of the major institutional investors in the US.

Davis Global

www.davisglobal.com

Advises on corporate governance issues and produce global proxy watch which is a two-page briefing on most important corporate governance developments around the world.

OMERS (Ontario Municipal Employers Retirement System) Canadian

www.omers.com/english/corporate-governance.html

One of the major institutional investors in Canada.

corpgov.net

www.Corpgov.net

This US website has lots of useful links to other sites.

International

International Corporate Governance Network

www.icgn.org

This site gives the corporate governance principles of the OECD. The international corporate governance network includes the ABI, CalPERS, TIAA-CREF etc.

OECD

www.oecd.org

Includes details on the Steering Group on Corporate Governance. The group, which includes delegates from all OECD member countries, guides and co-ordinates the Organisation's work on corporate governance. An important part of its work is to oversee the global outreach activities. These activities are carried out in co-operation with the World Bank, and also aim to encourage the use and implementation of the OECD Principles of Corporate Governance in non-member countries.

Glossary

A

ABI Guidelines Principles and guidelines on executive remuneration covering overall remuneration and incentive plans, published by the Association of British Insurers.

Accounting Standards Board (ASB) The body which sets accounting standards in the UK.

Annual bonus plan A variable annual incentive plan where the amount earned depends on the level of payout, which varies according to performance measured over one year or less.

B

Basic salary Either the basic salary in the emoluments table, or the basic salary that will become effective in the next financial year, as disclosed in the annual reports and accounts.

Binomial model A financial option pricing model to estimate the expected value of share-based payments using variables such as dividend yield, exercise period, exercise price, market price and share price volatility. The model is used to value executive share options and other long-term incentives; unlike the Black Scholes model, it takes into account the fact that executive share options have multiple exercise dates.

Black-Scholes model A financial option pricing model to calculate the expected value of share-based payments using variables such as dividend yield, exercise period, exercise price, market price and share price volatility. The model assumes that executive options can be exercised at only one point in time, and therefore may not be appropriate to estimate the expected value of executive options.

C

Co-investment plan An incentive plan whereby participants commit personal funds and are eligible to receive a 'matching' award from the company that is typically linked to their original investment and long-term performance of the company.

Combined Code (or the Revised Combined Code) Corporate governance recommendations combining the original Combined Code with the recommendations of the Higgs, Smith and Turnbull reports. The Combined Code is appended to the Listing Rules of the London Stock Exchange.

Comparator group A group of companies that are selected according to size, sector, geographic spread, and used for the purpose of measuring relative performance or to benchmark total remuneration packages of executives in a company.

Corporate bond yield A bond issued by a corporation which carries no claim to ownership and pays no dividends. Payments to bondholders have priority over payments to shareholders

D

Deferred annual bonus plan Variable incentive plan with performance/restrictions measured over a period of one year or less and where payment of the bonus earned is deferred for a further period of time. The deferred element (e.g. deferred shares) may be matched by the company (matching shares).

Deferred shares The proportion of the deferred annual bonus plan that is paid in shares that are deferred over a period of time.

Defined benefit pension plan A pension plan where the rules of the plan define the benefits that are payable and with contributions made at a level needed to provide these benefits. The most popular type of defined benefit pension plan is a final salary scheme.

Defined contribution pension plan A pension plan where the arrangement with participants is for a predetermined level of contributions to be made, with benefits provided on a money purchase basis.

Department of Trade and Industry (DTI) The government department in charge of regulating trade and industry in the UK.

Dilution limits The limits to the number of shares a company may issue under its equity-based incentive plan. The limits typically refer to an overall number of shares that may be issued at any given time; for example, 10 per cent of issued share capital over a ten-year period.

Directors' Remuneration Report Regulations 2002 Regulations that require all companies which are listed in the UK or any other EU state, or on the New York Stock Exchange or NASDAQ, to include a detailed report on directors' remuneration in the annual report; and put a resolution on the report to shareholders at each annual general meeting.

Discounted options Share options with an exercise price lower than the prevailing market price at the time of grant.

Double dipping If referring to an executive, the term is usually used to indicate that that person participates in more than one kind of share incentive arrangement (e.g. award of performance shares and grants of share options are made to the same executives in the same year) with each having similar performance conditions.

E

Earnings cap An Inland Revenue limit introduced by the 1989 Finance Act, stating the salary limit that is classed as pensionable earnings.

Earnings per share (EPS) A common measure of performance for share option plans. A number of EPS variations exist, such as diluted EPS, normalised EPS, EPS before or after exceptional items, and any combination of these.

Economic value added/economic profit (EVA) A measure of performance calculated by subtracting a charge for shareholders' capital and borrowing from a company's operating profits.

Exercise period The period of time over which an option or a share award may be 'traded in'.

Exercise price The price a holder of an option must pay to exercise it.

Expected value The present value of the sum of all the various possible outcomes at vesting or exercise of awards. This will reflect the probabilities of achieving these outcomes and also the future value implicit in these outcomes.

F

Final salary *See* **defined benefit pension plan.**

Financial Accounting Standards Board (FASB) US accounting body.

Financial Reporting Standard 17 (FRS 17) The requirements for accounting for retirement benefits in company accounts.

Financial Reporting Standard 20 (FRS 20) The new requirements for accounting for share-based payment in company accounts.

Fixed interest stock (or a corporate bond) The income you get is stable and corporate bonds aim to provide investors with a reliable and regular income.

Fixed pay A pre-determined set amount of money payable to an employee, for example basic salary.

FTSE 100 An index, produced by the FTSE Group, containing the 100 largest companies by market capitalisation listed on the London Stock Exchange.

Funded Unapproved Retirement Benefits Scheme (FURBS) A funded unapproved occupational pension scheme.

H

Higgs Report Derek Higgs led a short independent review of the role and effectiveness of non-executive directors in January 2003. A report was subsequently published and some of its recommendations included in the Combined Code and also appended as the Higgs Recommendations.

I

IAS 19 Sets out how employee benefits should be accounted for, except those to which IFRS 2 share-based payments apply.

IFRS 2 International Financial Reporting Standard introduced by the IASB that sets out how share-based payments should be accounted for.

Institutional shareholders/guidelines Some institutional investors (e.g. pension funds, insurance companies) have issued their own guidelines, (e.g. Morley, Legal & General, Hermes), outlining their approach to various issues including CSR, corporate governance and executive remuneration.

Institutional Voting Information Service (IVIS) Recommendation service for company AGMs/EGMs operated by the ABI. The service uses a system of colour coding to denote the ABI's overall view (i.e. red, amber, green, blue).

Institutional Shareholder Services (ISS) US provider of proxy voting and corporate governance services. The ISS and the NAPF have formed the joint venture RREV (*see below*).

International Accounting Standards Board (IASB) An institution whose aim is to harmonise accounting standards across the world.

'In the money' Share options with an exercise price lower than the current share price.

L

Lifetime allowance A new limit on individual pension pots included in the government's tax simplification proposals. From April 2006, pension funds valued in excess of that limit will suffer a taxable charge of 55 per cent.

Long-term cash plan Long-term incentive plan which ultimately pays out in cash and not in shares.

Long-term incentive plans (LTIP) Incentive plans other than share option plans where the performance period is longer than one year. Common types of LTIP are performance share plans and share matching plans.

M

Matching shares Conditional shares awarded whose value at award is based on the value of the deferred shares. Matching shares may be subject to further performance conditions that are measured over three years from the date of award.

Money purchase plan *See* defined contributions pension plan.

N

National Association of Pension Funds (NAPF) A UK body representing pension fund managers and trustees. The NAPF operates a joint voting service with ISS, termed RREV.

NED Non-executive director.

Nil-cost option Share option with nominal or zero exercise price (essentially a free share).

O

Other executive director Any main board position other than chief executives, finance directors and executive chairmen. This typically includes operational directors, functional directors, chief operating officers, and deputy chairmen.

'Out of the money' (or 'underwater') Share option with an exercise price higher than the current share price.

P

Performance condition A target, set at the outset of an LTIP or option grant, the attainment of which is required for the award/option to vest. Often relate to company performance and are related to a performance measure, or a combination of several performance measures, such as TSR and EPS.

Performance share plan (PSP) A type of LTIP in which participants are allocated shares, the vesting of which is subject to the satisfaction of performance targets, typically measured over three years.

Personal pension An arrangement under which an employee can make his or her own pension provision.

Potential value Illustrated values of awards depending on different share prices/ performance outcomes.

R

Research Recommendations Electronic Voting (RREV) A service providing proxy analysis and voting recommendations. The service is provided by a joint venture bringing together the NAPF and ISS.

Restricted shares A conditional allocation of free shares, with vesting restrictions which are time-based and/or subject to continued employment.

Retail Price Index (RPI) Measurement of the monthly change in the average level of retail prices in the UK, normally of a defined group of goods.

Retesting When a performance condition allows for performance to be remeasured if the original performance target is not met. Retesting may be allowed from a 'fixed-base' or may be over a rolling period (rolling retesting).

Return on capital employed (ROCE) Performance measure of overall efficiency in using available resources to generate profit.

Rolling retesting Method of measuring a performance condition over a period of fixed length (usually three years), but allowing that period to roll over any fixed window in the life of an option or LTIP award (e.g. from year three to six, or four to seven, or five to eight, etc.).

S

Share appreciation rights (SAR) An arrangement similar to a share option, but where holders are entitled to receive the intrinsic value only, paid in cash or equity, rather than the full amount of the equity.

Share option A right to buy a share some time in the future at a price specified at the outset. Share option plans are a common type of long-term incentive.

Sliding scale vesting Calibration of the vesting of a conditional award so that different proportions of award vest on a straight-line basis between performance levels.

Smith Guidance A committee, chaired by Sir Robert Smith, which was set up in order to clarify the role and responsibilities of audit committees. The findings of the report are now appended to the Combined Code as the Smith Guidance.

SOX/Sarbanes Oxley Act US legislation which has come into force to protect investors by improving accuracy and reliability of corporate disclosures made pursuant to US securities law.

T

Total shareholder return (TSR) Share price growth assuming dividends are reinvested.

Turnbull Report The abbreviated name given to guidance provided by the Institute of Chartered Accountants in England and Wales to enable UK companies to implement the internal controls required by the Combined Code on Corporate Governance. The Turnbull Guidance is appended to the Combined Code.

U

Underwater options Share options with an exercise price higher than the current share price.

Unfunded unapproved retirement benefits scheme (UURBS) An unfunded unapproved occupational pension scheme.

Index

INDEX